THE WORKING LIFE

A Medieval Monk

THE WORKING LIFE

A Medieval Monk

TITLES IN THE WORKING LIFE SERIES INCLUDE:

An Actor on the Elizabethan Stage

The Cavalry During the Civil War

A Colonial Craftsman

A Colonial Farmer

A Renaissance Painter's Studio

A Sweatshop During the Industrial Revolution

THE WORKING LIFE

A Medieval Monk

JAMES BARTER

LUCENT BOOKS®

THOMSON
™
GALE

San Diego • Detroit • New York • San Francisco • Cleveland • New Haven, Conn. • Waterville, Maine • London • Munich

LIBRARY OF CONGRESS CATALOGING-IN-PUBLICATION DATA

Barter, James, 1946-
    A medieval monk / by James Barter.
      v. cm. — (The working life series)
Includes bibliographical references (p.) and index.
Contents: Men who prayed—Training young men to become monks—Spiritual labor—
Running a monastery—Scholars—Artists and musicians—Traveling monks—Hermit
monks.
    ISBN 1-59018-478-5
  1. Monasticism and religious orders—Juvenile literature. 2. Church history—Middle
Ages, 600–1500—Juvenile literature. [1. Church history—Middle Ages, 600–1500.
2. Monastic and religious life.] I. Title. II. Series.
    BX2432.3.B37 2004
    271'.0094'0902—dc21
                                                                    2003006911

CONTENTS

FOREWORD

"The strongest bond of human sympathy outside the family relations should be one uniting all working people of all nations and tongues and kindreds."
Abraham Lincoln. 1864

Work is a common activity in which almost all people engage. It is probably the most universal of human experiences. As Henry Ford, inventor of the Model T said, "There will never be a system invented which will do away with the necessity of work." For many people, work takes up most of their day. They spend more time with their coworkers than with family and friends. And the common goals people pursue on the job may be among the first thoughts that they have in the morning, and the last that they may have at night.

While the idea of work is universal, the way it is done and who performs it vary considerably throughout history. The story of work is inextricably tied to the history of technology, the history of culture, and the history of gender and race. When the typewriter was invented, for example, it was considered the exclusive domain of men who worked as secretaries. As women

workers became more accepted, the secretarial role was gradually filled by women. Finally, with the invention of the computer, the modern secretary spends little time actually typing correspondence. Files are delivered via computer, and more time is spent on other tasks than the manual typing of correspondence and business.

This is just one example of how work brings together technology, gender, and culture. Another example is the American plantation slave. The harvesting of cotton was initially so cumbersome and time consuming that even with slaves its profitability was doubtful. With the invention of the cotton gin, however, efficiency improved, and slavery became a viable agricultural tool. It also became a southern tradition and institution, enough that the South was willing to go to war to preserve it.

The books in Lucent's Working Life series strive to show the intermingling of work, and its reflection in culture, technology, race, and gender. Indeed, history viewed through the perspective of the average worker is both enlightening and fascinating. Take the history of the typewriter, mentioned above. Readers today have access to more technology than any of their historical counterparts, and, in fact, though they would find the typewriter's keyboard familiar, they would find using it a bore. Finding out that people spent their days sitting over that machine (with no talk of carpal tunnel syndrome!) and were valued if they made no typing errors because corrections were cumbersome to make and, in some legal professions, made documents invalid, is an interesting story that involves many different aspects of history.

The desire to work is almost innate. As German socialist Ferdinand Lassalle said in the 1850s, "Workingmen we all are so far as we have the desire to make ourselves useful to human society in any way whatever." Yet each historical period offers a million different stories of the history of each job and how it was performed. And that history is the history of human society.

Each book in the Working Life series strives to tell the tale of these anonymous workers. Primary source quotes offer veracity and immediacy to each volume, letting the workers themselves tell their stories. In addition, thorough bibliographies tell students where they can find out more information, and complete indexes allow for easy perusal of the text. While students learn about the work of years gone by, they gain empathy for those who toil and, perhaps, a universal pride in taking up the work that will someday be theirs.

MEN WHO PRAYED

During the European Middle Ages, a period roughly between A.D. 500 and 1400, few thoughts occupied people's minds more than the uncertainty of whether heaven or hell awaited their souls. Those passionate about reaching heaven, were required to perform *opus Dei,* Latin for "the work of God." This included meeting obligations such as feeding and housing the poor, attending church services, praying daily, and caring for the sick and dispossessed.

The motivation for performing as many works of God as possible before dying was to increase one's chances for reaching heaven. Ordinary village people, however, working twelve-hour days in their grain fields, milking barns, or village shops, while raising families, had little time or money to commit to performing the works of God.

The Catholic Church understood this dilemma. To provide spiritual assistance for common people, it created an entire class of career employees within the church who dedicated their lives to prayer and to providing additional works of God for the working class. Those holding high positions, such as the pope, cardinals, and bishops, attended to the bureaucratic responsibilities of organizing its thousands of churches throughout Europe, its millions of followers, and its vast property. Others, such as lower-level priests, interacted directly with townspeople by providing for the needy and performing Sunday mass, marriages, confessions, baptisms, last rites, and funerals. Monks, however, occupied a unique rank within the medieval church; they were the men who prayed.

Prayer was a full-time commitment. Every waking hour focused on it. Prayer took many forms and involved complex rules that extended far beyond modern notions of prayer. To medieval monks, prayer was an obligation that permeated all aspects of their work. Unlike all other medieval professions, the job of monks did not begin in the morning and end with the setting sun as they went home. Monks had no private homes to go to, and they had job-related obligations every waking hour. In this regard, their job never ended.

Commitment to intense prayer demanded that monks live ascetic lives. They lived in isolation to avoid the distractions of marriage, family, business, personal pleasure, and other forms of social interaction. Such reclusion was rooted in dozens of biblical stories describing the lives of St. Mark, John the Baptist, and Christ, each of whom isolated himself from society for long periods of time in order to achieve a higher level of spirituality. Ascetic lives also included self-denial, the rejection of

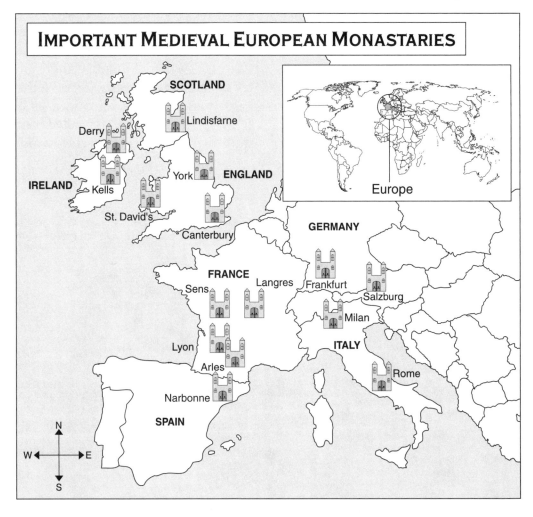

IMPORTANT MEDIEVAL EUROPEAN MONASTARIES

normal comforts such as comfortable clothes, warm meals, and soft beds. The saying most often quoted by monks to explain their self-denial was Christ's comment, "If you would be perfect, go, sell what you possess and give to the poor, and you will have treasure in heaven; and come, follow me."[1]

All officials within the church practiced various forms of social and personal asceticism but none as harsh as monks. St. Jerome, one of the early monks, made this distinction between the lives of monks and priests when conversing with another monk, Paulinius of Nola:

If you wish to perform the office of a priest, then live in cities and townships, and make the salvation of others the gain of your soul. But if you desire to be called a monk, which is solitary, what are you doing in cities, which are after all the dwelling places not of solitaries, but of the many?[2]

Medieval monks had three choices of how they could practice intense prayer and asceticism. In the most rigorous form, monks lived as hermits in underground burrows beneath desert sands and in other secluded places. The life of a hermit monk, without any social interaction, was so difficult that most monks preferred to join other monks to live and pray in walled communities called monasteries, which

A fifteenth-century painting shows monks gathered in prayer. The life of the medieval monk centered around a routine of fervent prayer.

were scattered throughout Europe. Monasteries provided a social structure for monks, yet they continued to work and pray, isolated from towns and villages. The third type of monk lived and worked while traveling the roads of Europe.

Remarkably little evidence of monkery remains in modern Europe. Although hundreds of monasteries are still scattered about the continent, only a few continue to ring bells summoning monks to prayer, meals, and religious services. Handfuls of monks can still occasionally be seen wearing their traditional garb in monasteries, although their numbers and influence have declined dramatically over the past six hundred years. Nonetheless, medieval scholars and historians look back and marvel at the tens of thousands of monks who lived Spartan lives in prayer and contemplation. How these people conducted their unusual lives, largely isolated from the rest of the world, and what they contributed to European culture is a compelling and extraordinary story.

CHAPTER 1

TRAINING YOUNG MEN TO BECOME MONKS

Being a monk during the Middle Ages was unlike any other job. Monks living in monasteries across Europe worked under conditions dramatically different from all other workers. Living in isolated monasteries remote from village and family life, unmarried and celibate monks understood the constant need to replenish their population by finding new recruits to replace old ones as they passed away.

One of the more delicate duties of the abbot, the highest-ranking monk in any monastery, was to locate new members for their brotherhood of monks. Newcomers were of two types: adult males who willingly came to monasteries after renouncing their past lives with family and friends, called *conversi,* from the Latin word meaning "to convert or turn their lives around," and young boys between the ages of five and seven who had no choice in the matter. These young boys, who were brought to the monasteries by their parents, were called oblates from the Latin word describing someone who has been "offered up." These oblates spent their youth growing up in the monasteries, awaiting their ordination as full-fledged monks. This period might last until they were about fifteen years old.

Oblates were of far greater interest to the monastery than the *conversi* because older monks knew that these young boys would grow up within the walls and develop deeper loyalties to the monastery. Consequently, from the very start, these oblates worked hard to learn the duties of monks, performing menial work around the monastery and studying to learn Latin and a variety of other academic skills. At the same time, the abbot and his senior staff of monks understood that they too had much hard work ahead of them to develop the young boys into high-quality monks who would carry on the tradition of their predecessors dating back to biblical times.

OBLATES AS STUDENTS

Medieval theologians believed that young oblates required a thorough education. Oblates were expected to be the future intellectual and moral elite of the monastery, and so they had much to learn. The ninth-century French abbot and writer St. Hildemar, one of the few respected abbots who wrote rules governing life and conduct in monasteries, required oblates to be well versed in Latin grammar and exposition, mathematics, theology, and singing. It was his contention that literacy in Latin and French was a prerequisite for ordination as a monk. To that end, all oblates spent some part of each day being educated by monks who were called *magistri* (from the Latin word for teachers).

ᴥ THE RULE ᴥ

The Rule of St. Benedict was the most influential and widely accepted set of rules for governing monastic life in Medieval Europe. The Rule, which was written in Italy about 530, was based on earlier compilations of rules for monastic life that came to be accepted within monasteries throughout Western Europe. St. Benedict compiled his Rule because he perceived the necessity for a permanent and uniform guideline for standardizing monks' conduct. His Rule replaced the arbitrary and variable choices available to the hermit monks, whom he strongly condemned as evil monks.

St. Benedict believed that a community of monks could function effectively only if each monk renounced his individualism in favor of conformity within the monastery. In that sense, the Rule functions to bind members of a monastery into a family unit in which each member shares all of the obligations and responsibilities necessary to keep the family alive.

Benedict's rule contains seventy-three chapters of varying length. Of the seventy-three chapters comprising the Rule, nine describe the duties of the abbot, thirteen regulate the worship of God, twenty-nine are concerned with discipline and the penal code, ten refer to the internal administration of the monastery, and the remaining twelve consist of miscellaneous regulations.

Within these chapters, he established the hierarchy of the monastery; the arrangements regarding prayer and work; details concerning the food, drink, and clothing of monks; punishments for violations of the Rule; and connections and relations with the outside world. His intent, which he makes very clear, was to provide reasonable guidance and encouragement, not to create an unreasonably difficult life nor to inflict harsh punishment.

St. Hildemar commented, "The children are ordered to busy themselves with their wax tables; that is, to practice their reading and writing."[3] According to historian Mayke de Jong, who published an academic paper titled "Growing Up in a Carolingian Monastery: Hildemar and His Oblates,"

church fathers, and the lives of the saints. They were encouraged to speak Latin among themselves in order to improve their understanding of the texts they read. This would also help them formulate dissertations in Latin, and to sharpen their intellects.[4]

Oblates read the Bible and commentaries on it, the works of the

In addition to studying Latin and the Bible, all oblates were required to

A monk teaches his oblate about the properties of mathematics in this fifth-century Italian painting.

IRREVERENT REASONS FOR BECOMING A MONK

Entering a monastery sometimes had little to do with devotion to prayer and furthering the spread of Christianity. For the very young oblates, those far too young to understand their actions, entering a monastery was the decision of parents whose motives most often were financial. If the family were very poor, they sent their sons to a monastery because they could not afford to feed and clothe them. If, however, the family were wealthy, they might send a younger son because an older son would someday inherit all the family wealth, known as the right of primogeniture, leaving nothing for the younger son. In such cases, wealthy parents were willing to pay a considerable amount of money to a monastery in exchange for accepting their son.

Men beyond their teenage years entered a monastery for a variety of reasons. Most were trying to avoid personal problems. On occasion, some convicted of minor civil crimes were remanded over to a monastery by a judge.

Abbots were not always obligated to accept criminals, but very often it proved lucrative. Courts offered life in a monastery only to those willing to relinquish all property and money to the monastery. For many men during the Middle Ages, choosing the monastery and poverty was a far better choice than trying to survive in the despicable conditions of most prisons.

Other men were escaping personal obligations to families, business partners, and the military. Some were in search of medical assistance. Historian Peter Speed notes in his book *Those Who Prayed,* "Many were drawn to the order [monasteries] by need, such as sickness, poverty, prison, shame for some fault, peril of death. . . . One man committed a theft, though a small one, against his master. He was caught by the servants and felt such shame that he fled from the world to a monastery. Another youth seduced a nun; and urged by shame and fear alike, he fled to a monastery."

read, study, and memorize the rules governing their particular monasteries. In most monasteries, this required the study of either St. Benedict's Rule or that of St. Hildemar. This requirement was emphasized for two reasons: First, knowing the rules governing conduct within a monastery led to an understanding of right and wrong; second, it established unity within the monastic community.

DAILY WORK ACTIVITIES

Oblates were expected to participate in one of many daily work activities. Since most oblates were quite young, the jobs chosen suited their ages. They were expected to attend some of the prayer sessions, but not all of them, and at least one of the major daily church services called Masses. Their attendance was expected at the *capitulum,* an occasional gathering for all members of the monastery during which the community listened to lectures, assigned tasks, discussed problems of concern to the entire community, and disciplined disobedient monks.

As to performing work to support the monastery, most abbots saw the kitchen, the dining hall, and the chapel as three of the best locations for oblates to contribute their energies several hours each day. Help was always needed, and there were many tasks suitable for young boys, including assisting cooks, waiting on tables, and singing in the choir.

COOKS AND WAITERS

Preparing meals was an ongoing job, and it was supervised by one senior monk called the cellarer. All oblates were required to participate in preparing meals in the kitchen, as St. Benedict indicated, "Let brethren serve each other so that no one be excused from the work in the kitchen, because greater merit and more charity is thereby acquired." Those who served the meals probably had few complaints because St. Benedict also stipulated that they should receive extra food: "An hour before meal time let the weekly servers receive each a cup of drink and a piece of bread over the prescribed portion."[5]

Meal preparation, generally twice a day depending upon season and location, included the constant chores of chopping, mixing, cooking, and cleaning. The youngest of the oblates received the job of carrying all needed ingredients into the kitchen: fresh vegetables from the garden; water from the well; wheat from the granary; cheese, eggs, and occasionally meat from the underground cold room; wine and beer from the cellar; and armfuls of wood for the fireplace from the chopping yard.

The middle-aged oblates, those between ten and twelve, took charge of general cleanup in the kitchen. These tasks were critical to control vermin such as rats and cockroaches that were considered pests in the kitchen. Cleaning included the thorough washing of all wood and ceramic mixing bowls, cast-iron cooking pots, wood counters, stirring utensils, and knives. Following the preparation of each meal, the floors were thoroughly swept, scrubbed with water, and dried with rags that were subsequently hung outdoors to dry. Cleaning the kitchen also included more than just washing floors, pots, and pans. St. Benedict stipulated that those finishing and those beginning their weekly cleaning stints must also "Wash the feet of all."[6]

The oldest oblates took direction from the cellarer for the more complicated and potentially dangerous jobs such as tending the fires, using knives for cutting, and mixing the ingredients for a variety of stews and soups, and the trickiest task of all, making dough and baking bread.

When bells signaled meal time, another set of oblates served food to the monks. Serving was a ritual that the boys conducted with bowed heads and in complete silence; no talking was allowed. First the boys gathered as a group at the entrance of the dining hall to await the arrival of their mas-

ters. Once all monks were seated, the oblates served the food and then took their places. Monks and oblates always ate on opposite sides of the table, never side by side, and the oblates were required to stand throughout the entire meal. One especially well-behaved oblate was always assigned to the abbot's table, which included senior monks and occasional guests. Following the meal, the oblates cleared the tables, gathered as a group and washed up, and accompanied their masters to the next activity for the day.

A fourteenth-century painting depicts young oblates in a philosophy class. In addition to their studies, oblates were responsible for many of the domestic chores of the monastery.

SINGING

A second primary responsibility of the young oblates was to sing in the choir. Singing was one of the few duties of the oblates that allowed them to play a major role in an activity. Singing was very important in monasteries because many forms of prayer required it. Prayers were sung daily along with psalms, canticles (short spiritual songs), and antiphons (short songs sung in response to a prayer recited by a monk).

At their young ages, the voices of oblates were very high, like that of a young girl, making them the only members of the monastic community capable of sounding different from the lower voices of mature men. For this reason, their role in prayer services was

A group of monks sings a hymn. The voices of young oblates lent an angelic quality to sacred music.

important. All oblates were ranked according to voice quality. Those at the very top of the list were often honored by being asked to sing solo excerpts and even to sing in place of senior monks who were absent. According to historian de Jong, "This indicates that the children had a separate hierarchy in the oratory in which they had their own positions just like the adults."[7]

Another reason the alto voices of young boys were revered is that it was believed in many monasteries that they had the "voices of angels." It was a common perception that prayers sung with high voices brought those praying closer to God. This notion was fueled by a statement made by St. Benedict in his Rule, who commented that a biblical prophet said,

> I will sing praise to Thee in the sight of the angels. Therefore, let us consider how it becomes us to behave in the sight of God and His angels, and let us so stand to sing, that our mind may be in harmony with our voice.[8]

Oblates were too young to perform their duties unsupervised. For this reason, the abbots of all monasteries appointed senior monks to function as custodians for the young boys. In some monasteries where many oblates entered each year, the job of monitoring them evolved into a major responsibility for the older monks.

CUSTODIAL SUPERVISION

All oblates were subject to constant supervision and diligent care by specially appointed monks called *custodia,* the Latin word for supervisors or custodians. The custodial monks were always senior men, but more important they were chosen by the abbot for their exceptionally superior moral character and high level of education. The principal charter of these custodians was to keep the boys focused on their jobs and studies, to prevent their youthful energies from disturbing the solemnity of the monastery, and to shield them from becoming victims of unwanted advances from older monks.

The ratio of custodians to oblates varied from monastery to monastery, but generally one monk supervised every two or three oblates. Such low ratios ensured that the young boys were constantly monitored. At no time did custodians permit oblates to be alone, to be in the company of other oblates without supervision, or to mingle unsupervised with monks. Whether the boys were involved in one of their many daily duties, walking across the monastery courtyard, playing on the grass, sleeping, or even using the latrine, none was beyond the watchful eyes of his custodian.

Close supervision was most dramatically demonstrated at bedtime. When the bells announcing the end of the day rang out across the monastery, the daytime custodial staff was relieved by the custodial staff called the "night watch." Those who had been with the oblates all day went to their dormitory to sleep while the night watch, which consisted of the oldest monks, arrived with lanterns to lead the oblates to the latrine. Even this evening ritual was performed the same way each night. Two of the monks with lanterns took the lead, followed by half of the oblates, then two more monks with lanterns, then the rest of the oblates, and finally two more monks with lanterns following up the rear.

Bedtime for the boys was not a time for sleep for the night watch. They remained awake all night with burning lamps to intervene if any of the boys became a nuisance, and, indeed, sometimes some did. Thirteenth-century records provide some insight into the boys' impertinent behavior at bedtime. One English document recorded,

> Whoever at bedtime has torn to pieces the bed of his companions, or hidden the bed clothes, or thrown shoes or pillows from corner to corner, or roused anger, or thrown the dormitory into disorder, shall be severely punished.[9]

The night watch also stayed awake all night to prevent any sort of sexual misconduct. Under no circumstances were any oblates or monks allowed to so much as touch one another in the dormitory. According to de Jong,

Obviously conduct in the dormitory was a sensitive point for a community that strove towards sexual asceticism. The monks were to avoid any sort of physical contact. Even seniors [monks] were not allowed to shake awake a sleeper. They had to tap against the foot of the bed in order to wake him. [10]

In addition to escorting and overseeing the safety of young oblates at night, the custodians also kept them focused on their daytime responsibilities. One of the times each day that this was particularly difficult was at 2 A.M. when the entire community filed into the chapel to sing prayers. Because the oblates played an important role as singers, they were not allowed to fall asleep while waiting to sing. To prevent them from falling asleep, custodians handed each oblate a heavy book to hold.

Proper shepherding of the young boys was often not sufficient to keep them focused on their duties and out of trouble. When unacceptable behavior threatened the calm of the monastery or an oblate's safety, senior monks added discipline to their list of responsibilities.

DISCIPLINE

The job of properly guiding the oblates through their daily routines was balanced with the job of properly disciplining them. The abbot was aware that life in the monastery was often

contrary to the unrestrained energy of the young boys and that the only way to keep them focused on their tasks was to apply reasonable discipline.

Living among the older and more highly disciplined monks was no easy task for capricious young oblates. Normal playfulness and irreverence of the oblates was commonly recorded by the older monks. Tricks were played on one another as would be common among any group of elementary schoolchildren. Tripping, poking, hitting, laughing, and teasing were apparently commonplace, as was an occasional blowing of pepper up someone's nose.

Older monks were aware of youthful behavior that violated the somberness of monastery life while at the same time understanding that all normal young boys would from time to time behave foolishly and disrespectfully. Striking a reasonable balance between discipline and leniency was recognized by St. Benedict, who reminded everyone, "Children are to be kept under discipline at all times and by everyone. Therefore, let the younger honor their elders, and the older love the younger." [11]

Discipline was most rigorously enforced during church services to prevent outbreaks of spontaneous silliness by the boys in the presence of the community of monks. One French monastery had obviously had its fill of misbehaving boys when it declared this discipline:

❧ DRAMATIC CONVERSIONS ❧

Adults wishing to renounce their secular lives in favor of undergoing conversion sometimes proceeded in dramatic fashion. Some were known to arrive at the gates of monasteries with bags filled with gold coins, ready to give up their wealth for the life of a monk. Others fleeing death sentences handed down by the courts begged hysterically at the gates to be admitted, promising to humbly serve the monastery if they were allowed to stay. One of the more celebrated conversions was recorded in 1230 when a German knight who had fought in the Crusades decided it was time to replace his armor in favor of a monk's habit. The following eyewitness account is recorded in Peter Speed's book Those Who Prayed:

A certain knight named Walewan, wishing to become a monk, rode to the monastery of Hemmenrode on his war-horse in full armor; and in full armor he rode into the cloister, and the porter led him down the middle of the choir, under the eyes of the whole community, who marveled at this new form of conversion. The knight then offered himself upon the altar of the Blessed Virgin, and, putting off his armor, he took the habit of religion, thinking it fit to lay down his earthly knighthood on the very spot where he proposed to become a knight of the Holy Ghost. Here, when the days of his novitiate were passed, he chose in his humility to become a lay-brother; and here he still lives, a good and religious man.

Whether they are standing or sitting in choir, let them not have their eyes turned aside to the people, but rather towards the altar; not grinning or chattering, or laughing aloud; not making fun of another if he does not read or sing the psalms well; not hitting one another secretly or openly. Those who break these rules will at once feel the rod. [12]

Such discipline for a minor infraction may sound extreme, yet it could get even worse. St. Stephen of Obazine had a reputation for his temper, as is indicated by this example of how he maintained discipline:

He corrected delinquents severely. If any raised his eyes but a little in church, or smiled but faintly, or slept but lightly, or dropped his book, or made any heedless sound, or chanted too fast or out of tune, or made an undisciplined movement, he at once received either a rod on his head or an open hand on his cheek, so loud that the blow rang in all men's ears. [13]

The significance for oblates of singing before the assembled community made for harsh discipline when singing did not go well. All oblates were expected to sing in tune and in time, but if they did not, harsh discipline might be meted out. Even St. Benedict, who understood the special needs of young boys, would not tolerate such negligence, as one of his rules suggests:

> If anyone while he sings a psalm, a responsory, an antiphon, or a lesson, makes a mistake, and does not humble himself there before all by making satisfaction, let him undergo a greater punishment, because he would not correct by humility what he did amiss through negligence. Let all children be beaten for such a fault. [14]

Discipline could take many other forms besides the corporal punishment of the rod or hand. Abbots were known to use food as a way of rewarding good behavior or punishing unacceptable behavior. St. Hildemar was known to allow obedient oblates to approach the abbot's table and to eat a small amount of choice food prepared for special guests, whereas troublemakers might be shamed by being made to sit alone at a dinner table without a plate of food.

The work of the young boys and their custodians to prepare each new generation of monks was an important and necessary task to ensure the continuation of each monastery. It was not, however, the main task within a monastery. Above all else, the charter of each monastery was to provide both spiritual and physical labors for the well-being of the monastic community.

CHAPTER 2

SPIRITUAL LABOR

Monks understood that spiritual labor was their most important responsibility. The complexity of spiritual work went far beyond prayer that is most commonly associated with their profession. Monks also defined spirituality by emulating the life of Christ whose principal teachings revolved around providing charity for the poor and around suffering by denying oneself personal comforts. The importance of suffering was illustrated by Christ's birth in a stable manger, his wearing one simple, unwashed robe, walking barefoot, fasting for days at a time, and enduring a painful death on the cross while wearing a crown of thorns. Although suffering was not a job in the traditional sense of requiring the completion of some task, it was, nonetheless, an important obligation. The importance of suffering as a daily form of labor is underscored in this twelfth-century prayer:

In the midst of our suffering, God is with us, closer to us than we are to ourselves. . . . In the midst of our suffering as a result of our faithfulness to God, there truly is no better place for us to be.[15]

To stress the importance of the labors of prayer, charity for the poor, and suffering by way of self-denial, St. Benedict wrote rules emphasizing the importance of each and how each should be practiced on a daily basis.

SINGING PRAYERS

Prayer was one of the most important obligations for monks. Prayer was heavily stressed in biblical passages as well as by St. Benedict, who admonished each monk, "To apply one's self often to prayer and to confess one's past sins to God daily in prayer with sighs and tears, and to amend them for the future."[16]

In the sixth century, St. Benedict (center) compiled a set of rules for monks to use as guidelines for their way of life.

In many monasteries the first call for prayer began with the ringing of a bell at 2:00 A.M. The bell signaled the start of the "daily round," a term used to refer to each monk's daily routine. Day after day, week after week, the daily round hardly varied. Each monk rose from sleep already partially clothed. After covering his bed with a blanket, he hurried to find his seat in the chapel to answer the first of the day's seven calls to prayer, called "the offices."

The first of the offices was called matins and lauds. It was later followed by prime at 6:00 A.M., terce at 9:00 A.M., sext at noon, none at 3:00 P.M., vespers at sunset, and compline before retiring for the evening. The prayers and psalms sung at each office were appropriate for the time of day. Matins and lauds, for example, was prayer rejoicing in the gift of a new day, while compline was a time for singing prayers of thanksgiving at the end of a day.

Seven times a day the entire congregation filed into the chapel and spent a half hour singing a series of memorized psalms, chants, prayers, and other short spiritual songs. On holy days, such as those celebrating Easter, Lent, and Christmas, traditional prayers for those occasions were substituted. The singing was lead by a monk with the title of cantor, whose principal responsibility was determining what would be sung at each of the seven offices and

holy days. Often he would compose new prayers, write them on several pieces of smooth wood, and distribute them to be memorized.

Singing was performed a cappella, originally meaning "in the style of the chapel," but since chapel singing was always done exclusively by monks, the term evolved to describe singing without instruments. The absence of musical instruments spurred the creation of prayer in the form of chants that rose and fell in pitch and volume many times during a single prayer. Interspersed with the bass sounds of the monks were the alto voices of the young boys.

While the early morning singing of matins and lauds took place, a few

---

✒ DAILY SCHEDULE ✒

In the Middle Ages, the daily pattern of life for a monk was dictated by bells signaling each activity. The website Information Devon (www.devon.gov.uk) provides the following schedule for medieval monks at the Buckfast Monastery in England:

1:45 A.M.—Wake up
2:00 A.M.—Church service
3:30 A.M.—Sleep
4:00 A.M.—Church service
5:00 A.M.—Private reading and prayer
6:00 A.M.—Church service, then breakfast

7:00 A.M.—Work
8:00 A.M.—Church service
9:15 A.M.—Work
11:45 A.M.—Church service
12:00 P.M.—Midday meal
1:00 P.M.—Private reading and prayer
1:45 P.M.—Sleep
2:45 P.M.—Church service
3:00 P.M.—Work
5:45 P.M.—Meal
6:00 P.M.—Church service
7:15 P.M.—Private reading and prayer
7:45 P.M.—Church service
8:00 P.M.—Bed

monks had the job of wandering the chapel. Each carried a lamp to swing in the face of any person who might lapse back into a deep sleep. If swinging the lamp did not awaken a monk from slumber, the lamp was left at his foot as a sign, when he finally awoke, that he had been detected sleeping and that he would need to fall to his knees and beg for forgiveness. Following the singing, monks made their way back to their straw beds for an hour or so until the next bell awakened them for their next activity, which usually meant more prayer at Mass.

PRAYER AT MASS

Interspersed within the seven offices were two masses, one in the morning and the other in the evening. Each mass was a complex collection of prayers, ceremonies, and chants focusing principally on one particular spiritual event, the Eucharist, a Greek word meaning "a moment for giving thanks." This event celebrated a story in the bible in which it was believed Christ converted wine and bread into his blood and flesh during his last meal before he died.

Each mass was conducted by the abbot, who presided over all prayer and other spiritual traditions. As each monk entered the chapel, he dipped his fingers into a bowl of water that had been blessed by the abbot and preceded to his seat. Just before sitting down, he knelt on one knee to demonstrate his humility, a ritual known as genuflec-

tion, and he said a short, silent prayer. Following communal prayer directed by the abbot, the ritual of communion began.

Communion was the high point of the Mass. It was a ritual focusing on the tradition of the Eucharist that was intended to direct everyone's thoughts to the death and sacrifice of Jesus. During communion, the abbot held a cup of wine and a plate of bits of bread above his head and declared them the blood and body of Christ and welcomed all monks to come forward to drink from the cup and eat from the plate. Following this ritual, more prayers were spoken and each member of the community knelt down for a few minutes of private prayer before departing for the next commitment of the day.

Prayer was at the heart of each monastery but not to the exclusion of performing many charitable acts for the benefit of the poor and dispirited. In keeping with the teachings of Christ to help the dispossessed, all monasteries required their monks to help the needy local townspeople.

CHARITABLE WORKS

The concept of charitable works was captured within the Latin phrase *opus Dei*. Abbots embraced the notion of *opus Dei* by providing humanitarian aid to the local peasantry. Assisting this traditionally poor segment of Europe's population was perceived to be in keep-

A fifteenth-century painting depicts two monks in prayer. Medieval monks adhered to a daily schedule that included many hours of prayer.

ing with the biblical tradition of Jesus, who fed the poor, sheltered the homeless, and healed the sick. In this regard, charitable work, often called almsgiving, was one of the cornerstones of a monk's spiritual work. St. Benedict believed in it so strongly that he included it as a requirement in his Rule, "Let the greatest care be taken, especially in the reception of the poor, because Christ is received more specially in them." [17] Elsewhere in his Rule he writes, "Let him [the monk] provide for the sick, the children, the guests, and the poor, with all care." [18]

FEEDING THE POOR

Almsgiving occurred on a daily basis in most monasteries. Early in the morning after monks had finished their baking, a specific amount of bread was baked and designated as alms bread for the poor. In large monasteries this daily ritual required one monk, called the almoner, to organize the baking and distribution of the bread.

As the sun was rising, a somber procession of monks walked from the kitchen to the monastery gate carrying a prescribed amount of food—usually bread, beer, and occasionally cheese—to distribute to the local poor who gathered there. In addition to the bread, dinner scraps from the previous night were also sent out. Better-quality foods were also distributed on holy days when monks feasted and were able to share a greater variety of foods.

Historian Ludo J.R. Milis, in his book *Angelic Monks and Earthly Men: Monasticism and Its Meaning to Medieval Society,* describes one monastery in France of about fifty monks that daily dispersed fifty bread rolls made from four pounds of wheat and barley. The monks also dispersed beer, some cheese, and bacon. In comparison, the monks at Cluny, a much larger French monastery, made a daily dispersal of thirty-six pounds of bread. Regardless of the amount of food provided, it was never enough for everyone. According to the complaints of one of Cluny's abbots, Peter the Venerable, "There is always a crown of guests and the number of poor people is innumerable." [19]

❧ TRENCHERS ☙

Each day when bread was baked, any remaining loaves that were not eaten or distributed as alms to the poor were set aside to be used at a later time for trenchers. Without doubt, they were one of the more unusual features of monastery meals when used as plates to hold food. The word is derived from the French verb *trenchier* or *trancher,* meaning to cut, because the trencher was cut from a stale loaf of bread.

On occasion, burned bread might become trenchers. The cellarer often turned the job of baking bread over to older oblates, who from time to time either overheated the oven or failed to pay attention, leaving the loaves in the oven too long. When burned loaves were discovered by the cellarer, he sliced off the lower, burned half and set them aside for use as trenchers.

Trenchers were roughly four by eight inches and two inches thick. At many monasteries, two monks shared one trencher. When oblate servers brought them to the tables, monks ladled stews and thick soups onto them. While the filling was being eaten, the juices soaked into the trencher, slightly softening and flavoring it by the time it was finally eaten. Although everyone in the monastery ate from trenchers, the upper part of each loaf of bread, the softest part of the loaf, was always reserved for favored guests and the abbot and his senior staff.

On occasion, the trenchers disappeared from the table uneaten. Although this was against the rules, they were taken by monks and oblates, hidden in their habits, and eaten at a later time when hunger set in.

Providing food to the poor required a specific presentation. The monks presented the food in a humble manner, with heads bowed and never looking directly at the recipients. Such humility was intended to emphasize the unpretentiousness of their offerings and their respect for those receiving the food. In keeping with the sanctity of almsgiving, once a year during Lent the monks washed the feet of the poor. To further emphasize the spiritual value of almsgiving, the almoner entered the local village on a weekly basis in search of those not able to come to the monastery gate in the morning, and he fed them.

HOUSING THE DISPOSSESSED

Providing food was only one part of caring for the poor. More often than not, those who received food also needed shelter. In keeping with the spiritual obligation of charitable works, monks opened their monasteries to shelter the dispossessed. Peasant families rarely owned their own homes. And when crops failed, families often found themselves evicted. Abbots were sympathetic to these homeless people and worked to assist them by opening inns, called hospices, as safe places to shelter them. This gesture was very much in keeping with their notion of *opus Dei* and closely tied to the biblical story of the birth of Christ in the manger of a barn. According to historian C.W. Lawrence in his book *Medieval Monasticism,* a me-

dieval chronicler at Beaulieu monastery in France explained,

> The monks offered hospitality in the hospice each night to not more than thirteen poor men. On Christmas Eve, they were to give hospitality to as many poor people as there were monks in the monastery. [20]

Accommodating the poor placed an additional burden on the monks and oblates. Most large monasteries required monks to make hospice rooms ready to receive visiting poor. Dozens of simple rooms similar to the monks' dormitories were swept and cleaned each day. The mattresses were heavy muslin sacks stuffed full of straw and sewn tight. As these fell apart, monks sent the oblates to the fields to fetch fresh straw. Since disease was always a threat, oblates burned the old straw and occasionally sprinkled lime powder on the floors to kill germs.

A simple mass was added to the responsibilities of caring for the poor. Although the abbots did not allow the visitors to attend services with the monks, they did send a senior monk to offer communion.

A night's stay in the hospice might also include the alms of clothing. Several medieval sources note that barefoot paupers were sent away with monk's shoes, even though such sacrifice on the part of monks meant going barefoot the remainder of the year. Sacrificing their shoes was viewed as an act of great piety within the monasteries, and barefoot monks were honored by the abbot for their sacrifice. Others in need of proper clothing received shirts and robes made within the monastery.

In response to the plight of homeless children either abandoned by their parents or orphaned by their parents' deaths, monks opened orphanages to care for them. The job of the monks was to provide them with a place to sleep and eat in exchange for daily work. The monks had the additional responsibility of keeping the orphans separated from the oblates. Some of the more enlightened monasteries such as one in Athens during the eleventh century also required the monks to educate the children, as the writer Anna Comnena noted in her journal:

> The children who had lost their parents and were afflicted with the bitter evil of orphanhood he [emperor Alexius] distributed among his relations and others who, as he knew, led a well-conducted life, or sent them to the abbots of the holy monasteries with orders to bring them up, not as slaves, but as free children and allow them a thorough education and instruction in the Holy Writings. [21]

Spiritual duties extended beyond prayer and acts of charity to encompass the guiding principle of asceticism, more commonly known as the practice of self-denial. Honoring the many attributes of self-denial demanded a great deal of work on the part of its practioneers.

THE DUTY OF SELF-DENIAL

All monks pledged to lead lives emulating the life of Christ. One of their pledges that encompassed many of his teachings was to asceticism, which obligated each monk to live as close to poverty as possible and to understand that the suffering that came from poverty would bring them spiritually closer to God. Asceticism was based on the belief that far more could be learned from suffering than from a life of comfort and indulgence.

Participation in asceticism was considered part of each monk's daily obligation. One of the most respected monks who lived asceticism rigorously was St. Francis of Assisi, who lived in the late-twelfth and early-thirteenth century. His work of self-denial and discomfort was legendary, as this account of his duties in the thirteenth-century *Barnwell Chronicle* attests:

> St. Francis slept in his clothes by night, used rushes for a mattress and placed a rock under his head for a pillow, content with only the hair shirt which he wore during the day as a blanket. Thus he traveled barefoot in accordance with

the gospel . . . and stood dissociated from fleshly lust and drunken greed. [22]

In keeping with the example of St. Francis, abbots insisted that their monks demonstrate their commitment to asceticism in tangible ways that would validate their willingness to suffer as part of their job. Such examples of self-denial took form in their meager meals, minimal hygienic care, and suffering while asleep.

MEAGER MEALS

Medieval monks ate meager, plain meals in keeping with their vows of asceticism. Food was viewed as a necessity for sustaining life but not as something to be enjoyed. For that reason, Spartan meals were usually prepared without any spices, although a small number of monasteries permitted the occasional use of salt, pepper, and mustard.

Frequency of meals and types of food varied from country to country, but most monks could anticipate only one meal a day during the winter when cold weather confined them to indoor activities. When the weather warmed, however, monks could count on two meals a day—and on some rare occasions, three—to replenish calories burned while gardening, well-digging, and repairing buildings.

Monks were restricted to vegetarian meals of fruits and vegetables

The austere lifestyle of self-denial practiced by St. Francis became the model for monastic living.

ᴇᴛɪQUETTE AT THE TABLE

Monks ate in silence but not always with manners. Hugh of St. Victor, one of the leading theologians of the twelfth century, wrote widely about issues of the church and monasteries. One short essay, "Rules for Novices," provided monks a set of rules for everyday living. Included in it is an observation about terrible dining etiquette that Hugh found particularly offensive. The following excerpt is found in Peter Speed's book Those Who Prayed:

At one and the same moment they [monks] crumble their bread, poor wine into cups, spin the dishes around on the table; and, like a king about to assault a beleaguered city, they doubt where they should make their first assault, since they would rush upon every point at once.

Some in their haste to empty the dishes, wrap in the table-clothe, or even cast upon it, fragments of crust still dripping with fat or gravy. Others, as they drink, plunge their fingers halfway into the cup. Others, wiping their greasy hands on their frocks, turn again to handle the food. Others fish for their pot-herbs [vegetables] with their fingers, instead of with a spoon, trying, it would seem, to wash their hands and refresh their bellies in one and the same broth. Others dip into the dishes their half-gnawed crusts and bitten morsels, in their haste to make a sop [meal of bread and gravy] for themselves, plunging what their teeth have spared into the dish.

grown in their own gardens. In keeping with their vows of asceticism, the primary vegetables grown were those suitable for basic soups and thick stews. Most common were a small variety of peas, beets, carrots, and celery. Historian Peter Speed notes in his book *Those Who Prayed* that monks could have a sense of humor about the monotony of this diet. According to Speed, "It was said that dinner on four successive days was peas and pot-herbs [vegetables], pot-herbs and peas, peas with pot-herbs, and pot-herbs with peas."[23]

Bread was always the most important food of each meal and the most plentiful. Bread was generally described as being black and coarse and was served in one of two ways: either in one-pound loaves baked daily, one of which was give to each monk, or in the form of a trencher, a flat, thick piece of three-day-old leftover bread used as a plate. The hard trencher was placed directly on the table and covered with stew and vegetables. When the stew and vegetables were gone, the monks picked up the juice-soaked trencher and ate it as well.

Medieval writers reveal that some monasteries violated the rule of ascetic eating, and when they did, they were widely criticized. In 1200, for example, Gerald of Wales condemned a meal for the brethren at Canterbury, England, with considerable disgust:

> I felt as if I were sitting at a stage play or among the company of actors and buffoons. Six courses or more were laid on the table. . . . Vegetables were scarcely touched, in the face of so many kinds of fishes, roast and broiled, stuffed and fried—so many dishes tricked out by the cook's art with eggs and pepper—so many savory sauces to excite the appetite. . . . What would Paul the Hermit have said of this? Or Anthony? Or Benedict, father and founder of monastic life? [24]

MINIMAL HYGIENIC CARE

Monks lived most of their lives coated with body oils and dirt. Enduring

A group of monks gather at a table for a modest meal. Most monks ate simple vegetarian meals prepared with fruits and vegtables grown in their garden.

unpleasant health standards was viewed by monks as one of their jobs. Personal hygiene was viewed by most monks as an unnecessary indulgence and by others as sinful because it pampered their bodies. Experiencing the discomfort of an unbathed body rubbed raw from coarse clothing and unwashed hair itching from lice was viewed as being consistent with Christ's suffering in the desert where he lived for forty days without bathing. A disregard for body comforts was considered a sign of holiness because bathing was viewed as a distraction from the more important work of prayer.

Bathing at most monasteries was a rare event. St. Benedict recommended that it occur only three times a year: Christmas, Easter, and Pentecost. Yet, he added the proviso that those objecting could abstain from bathing for an entire year. When monks did bathe, all entered a bathhouse where a screen was set up for a few moments of rare privacy, but they had to endure a tub of cold water. In keeping with the view that monks ought to shun any sense of pleasure, historian C.W. Lawrence cites a medieval chronicler who warns, "When he [a monk] has sufficiently washed, he shall not stay for pleasure but shall rise, dress, and return to the cloister." [25]

A shave and haircut were no more comfortable than a bath. Monks did not wear full beards year round, nor did they shave on a daily basis. The cutting of beards was a ritual that occurred before specific holy days when all monks filed into a room for the event. The abbot removed razors and shaving bowls from a cupboard and handed them out to the monks sitting on long benches. When one monk completed his shave, he handed the razor and bowl to the next monk until all had shaved. At one monastery, St. Augustine's, the monks took turns shaving each other. However, as one chronicler pointed out, "The wounds they inflicted on each other's faces were so bad that Abbot Roger imported lay barbers to do the job." [26] Maintaining the monks' distinctive haircut, called the tonsure, required shaving the tops of their heads but merely trimming hair around the sides. This tonsure was done by one monk shaving the head of the other, and the style was not allowed to be altered.

SUFFERING WHILE ASLEEP

As part of their job, monks were required to suffer even in their sleep. Monks retired to bed between seven and eight o'clock in the evening, depending upon their location and the season. When the bells tolled the last hour of the day, all monks filed into a common dormitory without any partitions separating the sleeping men. They slept on straw mats or on wooden pallets covered with straw. They had a blanket, and rolled-up clothes

❧ SIGNS OF SILENCE ❧

The vow of silence was one of the more difficult vows to obey. Many medieval writers make references to the number of monks who continually failed to keep their tongues still. Over time the frustration drove monks to invent various forms of sign language that enabled them to communicate without uttering a single sound. Robert A. Barakat, in his book The Cistercian Sign Language: A Study in Non-Verbal Communication, *presents more than three hundred different basic signs plus several hundred more compound signs used by the Cistercian monks, with accompanying photographs and descriptions such as the following:*

Apple—Turn tip of little finger into open palm of hand.

Book—Place heels of hands together then open and close like a book.

Dead—Place tip of right thumb under chin raising it a bit.

Devil—Strike the forehead with tip of right forefinger several times.

Evening—Place tip of right forefinger over closed right eye.

Fish—Wag the hand sideways, in the manner of a fish tail.

Heart—With tips of both forefingers draw a heart over the heart.

Incense—Place two fingers in the two nostrils.

Mustard—Hold the nose in the upper part of the right fist and rub it.

Pray—Interlace fingers of both hands.

Sleeping—Put the right hand under the cheek and close the eyes.

Snake—Move the right forefinger forward in a zigzag motion.

Washing—Rub the right hand in the back of the left.

Work—Strike thumb side of left fist with little finger side of right fist repeatedly.

took the place of a proper pillow. A lantern burned all night long to discourage conversation and physical contact.

Monks were not allowed the comfort of pajamas; they continued to wear their habit, although it was commonplace to remove the cowl, a hood, and the scapular, a garment similar to an apron. Sleeping in their habit may have been a blessing during winter nights but certainly not during the summer in warmer locations near the Mediterranean Sea. The discomfort was made even worse at Cluny where the rules required monks to sleep completely covered at all times except for their feet and arms.

Asceticism was also applied to the amount of nightly sleep. St. Benedict was clear in his Rule that all monks ought to have no more than six hours of uninterrupted sleep at night unless they were ill. To prevent young monks from disturbing the older monks, St. Benedict recommended they be mixed in with older monks. "Let the younger brethren not have their beds beside each other, but intermingled with the older ones." [27]

The many forms of spiritual work that were associated with prayer, charitable works, and acts of asceticism were considered good for the soul. Keeping the monastery functioning, however, required more practical forms of work. To keep everyone fed, housed, and clothed, each monk was required to perform physical work.

CHAPTER 3

RUNNING A MONASTERY

All medieval monks were expected to contribute to the upkeep of the monastery. One of the basic obligations of monastic life according to St. Benedict was that each monk engage in some daily form of physical toil, *quia virtus est animae et corporis,* "which is good for mind and body."[28] Numerous medieval illuminated manuscripts depict monks wearing their traditional hooded robes and distinctive haircuts working in grain fields and chopping down forest trees. Depictions of monks standing in fields planting, cutting, and threshing grain suggest that agriculture was the primary physical labor of monks.

Work generally occupied seven hours a day during spring and summer and four to five hours a day for the remainder of the year. The importance of work went beyond the simple need for exercise. Everyone lending a hand diminished the need for outside assistance and made the monastery self-sufficient, a value embraced and expounded by St. Benedict:

> If it can be done, the monastery should be so situated that all the necessaries, such as water, the mill, the garden, are enclosed, and the various work arts may be plied inside of the monastery, so that there my be no need for the monks to go about outside, because it is not good for their souls. But we desire that this Rule be read quite often in the community, that none of the brethren may excuse himself of ignorance.[29]

WORKING THE LAND

Most monks, young and old, rose from their prayers following prime and at the command *"Ad opera manuum ibimus in hortum,"* "Let us now go to our manual work in the garden."[30] The monks then

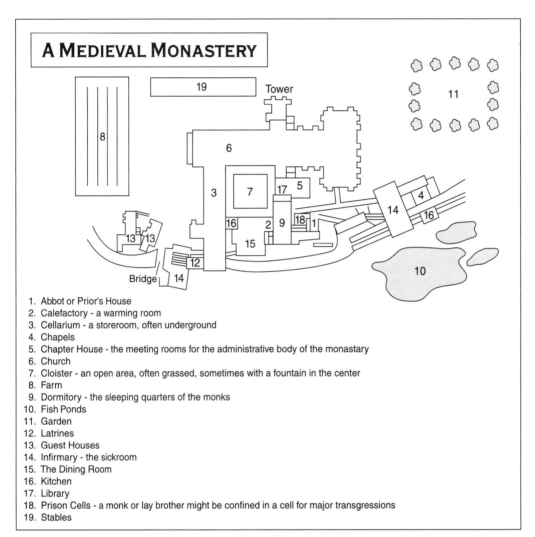

A MEDIEVAL MONASTERY

Tower

19

8

11

6

3   7   17 5

14   4

16   2 9 18 1   16

15

12

Bridge   14

10

1. Abbot or Prior's House
2. Calefactory - a warming room
3. Cellarium - a storeroom, often underground
4. Chapels
5. Chapter House - the meeting rooms for the administrative body of the monastary
6. Church
7. Cloister - an open area, often grassed, sometimes with a fountain in the center
8. Farm
9. Dormitory - the sleeping quarters of the monks
10. Fish Ponds
11. Garden
12. Latrines
13. Guest Houses
14. Infirmary - the sickroom
15. The Dining Room
16. Kitchen
17. Library
18. Prison Cells - a monk or lay brother might be confined in a cell for major transgressions
19. Stables

proceeded to the vegetable garden while singing psalms. Since gardens were both a place for growing food and a place of spiritual reverence, all bowed toward the east upon reaching the garden, and it was not until a prayer was recited that everyone picked up his tools and set to work.

Vegetable gardens were the principal source of food for the monastery. For this reason, gardens could be quite large, sometimes several acres, requiring constant care from early spring through late fall. During this seven-month period, monks could anticipate multiple crops of peas, squash, beets, tomatoes, carrots, lettuce, and celery because these vegetables grew and matured quickly in fertile soil. By staggering the time of plantings, monks enjoyed a bounty of all these fresh foods for at least seven months of the year.

Wielding simple wooden tools such as hoes, shovels, water bags made of animal skins, and wheelbarrows, monks busied themselves tending their crops. In the early spring, immediately fol-lowing spring thaw, monks turned the soil by pushing small plows mounted on a single wheel up and down the garden. The plow blade turned the soil, uprooting weeds while at the same time aerating deep soil for new crops. Robust crops required rich soil so

❧ A DISDAIN FOR MANUAL LABOR ❧

The requirement that all monks participate daily in several hours of manual labor did not sit well with all of them. There were always tasks to be performed in the fields and workshops of the monasteries, but toward the twelfth and thirteenth centuries some of the monasteries had managed to collect enough money to employ secular servants to perform many of the more menial and less desirable jobs. This turn of events was met with great enthusiasm by many monks who gradually favored the elimination of manual work in favor of more stimulating intellectual activities.

One of the reasons the change was so well received by many monks was that, toward the end of the Middle Ages, the tilling of soil and working with barnyard animals had become associated with the work of peasants and various servile crafts-men who were not the people with whom some of the more sophisticated monks wished to associate. One abbot, Peter the Venerable, quoted by C.H. Lawrence in *Medieval Monasticism,* went so far as to argue that "The delicate hands of my monks, who came from social classes unfamiliar with toil, are more suitably employed furrowing parchment with pens than plowing furrows in fields."

Many monks thought manual labor was beneath them, and preferred intellectual activities such as writing.

monks fertilized them with a mixture of ground-up fish remains, cow manure, and a sprinkling of sawdust to hold moisture. After the rows were planted, young oblates were given the task of using slings to chase off any birds that swooped in to eat the seed. The crops were then irrigated and harvested by hand as they matured.

A small number of monasteries had sufficient land to also grow grains used to make their breads. Monks charged with growing wheat, barley, or rye worked the same seven months as those tending the vegetable gardens, but the work was more complicated. First, monks hitched plows to oxen to turn the soil. Then they spread the seed, covered it using large rakes, and waited for the crop to mature. In the late summer, monks assisted by older oblates harvested the grain by first cutting it with long curved knives called scythes and then tying it into bundles called shocks. Older oblates then stacked and carried the shocks to a barn or granary where the grain was separated from the stalks by beating them on the ground. Finally the grain was placed in sacks and stored in a dry place.

Occasionally, unusual types of agricultural work were asked of monks to provide additional foods. At some monasteries, monks were required to tend bees that provided wax for church candles and honey to sweeten the food. Some monastery locations were suitable for monks to tend small fruit orchards. Other monasteries, particularly in France and Italy, were suited to grow grapes that were either eaten at mealtime or crushed and fermented into wine.

TENDING LIVESTOCK

Some monks tended to the livestock rather than working in the garden. Although meat was rarely eaten by the monks, an interesting assortment of livestock was raised for their meat and sold to neighboring towns. These same animals also provided a variety of milk by-products such as cheese and butter, and their skins were used by the monks.

The livestock that required the most work were the larger animals such as milk cows and sheep that needed to graze on wild grasses to sustain themselves. The milk cows were permitted to roam freely across the local meadows without fear of losing them because the pain of their udders swelling with milk motivated them to return to the monastery for milking each morning and night. When the cattle returned, they were milked by monks and the pails of milk placed in cool underground cellars for sale or to be made into cheese and butter for sale or trade with the local villagers.

Both cheese and butter were made by monks under the direction of the cellarer or his assistant, the subcellarer. Either monk saw to it that the thick cream floating at the top of the pail was

Monks harvest grain in this fifteenth-century painting. Most medieval monasteries included plots of land on which crops of fruit and grain were grown.

skimmed and placed in separate containers, one for cheese and the other for butter. Cream destined to become butter was transferred into wooden butter churns for conversion to butter. The butter churn was a two-foot-tall cylinder with removable top through which a small hole was drilled. Through the hole was placed a wooden plunger, which, when forced up and down rapidly, gradually thickened the cream into butter.

Making cheese was a trickier process. The milk and cream were first heated a short time and then either placed in the stomach of a recently killed goat or mixed with the stomach content removed from a goat. The bacteria from the stomach act to thicken the milk-and-cream mixture into curd, which monks then cut into small cubes and set in a vat in a warm place until the curd fell to the bottom; then the watery whey was drained off. Monks scooped

❧ MONASTIC FISHPONDS ❧

The general prohibition of eating meat from livestock meant that fish became a major source of protein in most monasteries. Large monasteries appointed one man, the *piscator,* Latin for "fisherman," whose sole responsibility was to provide the cellarer with weekly supplies of fresh fish.

The job of the *piscator* was not simple owing to the fact that few monasteries had sizeable rivers crossing their properties where fish could be caught. The sanctity of being a monk required most men to remain within the walls to perform most of their work, which made it impossible to leave the monastery on a daily basis to fish. On occasion, monks were allowed to barter commodities produced at the monastery such as cheeses, butter, and red meat in exchange for fish, but even this sort of trade oftentimes left the monks with old, smelly fish leftover from a long, hot day in the village marketplace.

To solve the problem, *piscators* learned a lesson from their Roman predecessors that involved building large fish ponds within the monastery walls that could be stocked with live fish. Such fish ponds that archaeologists have excavated reveal a fairly complicated stone and concrete structure built above ground. Their size depended on the size of the community, but some of the largest were twenty-five feet wide by fifty feet long and three to four feet deep. It was the job of the *piscator* to stock the pond either by catching the fish himself once a week or by bartering goods for live fish. In either case, his job included feeding the fish grain from the monastery granary and, if possible, running a trickle of freshwater into the tank to keep the water fresh.

When the *piscator* was asked by the cellarer to supply fresh fish for a meal, he waded into the tank, deployed a wide net, and walked the length of the tank trapping the fish until he had enough for the meal. The freshness of fish was of such importance to the cellarer that the *piscator* was the only food-related worker allowed to bring his catch directly across the central corridors of the monastery to the kitchen, to ensure its freshness. All others carried their foods around the perimeter of the courtyard.

together slabs of curd, added salt and mild flavoring, and pressed them into forms for aging. Once the cheese was aged, it was used as trade for items monks could not make.

Tending the sheep was more difficult than caring for cattle. Sheep were not compelled to return to the monastery as were the cows, forcing monks to construct pens called "folds" to contain them at night. Sheep provided a second problem because when they grazed, they nipped the grass at ground level and killed the blades. To avoid denuding vast stretches of meadowlands, monks took turns keeping the sheep moving and guiding them to fresh grass that allowed recently grazed meadows to rejuvenate themselves. Then, as the sun set, the monks drove the sheep back to the folds near the monastery.

The surplus of grains and meats came in handy as commodities that monks could barter for other needed goods that they could not produce. It was also useful to keep a surplus on hand to help feed a constant stream of travelers who used monasteries as inns and taverns.

SHELTERING TRAVELERS

In stark contrast to the principles of asceticism and charitable works for the destitute, monasteries functioned as hotels and inns for medieval European travelers. Monks were obligated, as part of their *opus Dei,* to accommodate paying travelers for a night's stay re-gardless of their social or economic status.

A large monastery might maintain three or four different levels of accommodations, depending upon the social rank of the guests. The guests varied widely, from traveling nobility in their carriages, merchants selling their wares on donkeys, visiting monks from neighboring monasteries, pilgrims traveling to visit holy shrines on foot throughout Europe, to simple peasants.

Many wealthy lords and ladies enjoyed the quiet solemnity of a monastery, a healthy dinner, and a sparse yet warm, clean bedroom. Well-heeled travelers preferred such accommodations to the often cantankerous and rowdy behavior they might find staying at commercial inns in towns or even in the homes of noble friends and relatives.

To accommodate the expectations of such a varied collection of overnight guests, one senior monk was assigned the job of supervising a group of younger monks. These monks, often made up of older oblates and young novitiates, were responsible for preparing rooms, carrying baggage, and stabling horses. Preparing the rooms for the wealthier travelers was a time-consuming task because they were the largest, most elaborate, and most comfortable guest houses in the monastery. In some cases, each had a fireplace that the oblates banked with wood each day to keep it warm at night. Furthermore, oblates swept wooden floors and filled

An illustration from a French manuscript depicts a pilgrimage to an abbey. Many medieval monasteries served as inns for weary travelers.

candleholders with new candles. The most demanding and tiresome job was to prepare mattresses made of goose down. The monks had to move the mattresses outside, beat them with a rod to fluff up the down, and return them to their rope supports that were then twisted tight to provide a firm foundation. Preparing rooms for frugal travelers was more easily accomplished because these visitors stayed in very small, simple rooms called almonries where several shared a room and slept on straw mattresses.

Meals for the wealthier guests and visiting monks made for additional work for the cellarer and his staff. The meals for these guests were superior in quality to what the monks received, and for this reason, the cellarer prepared the finer guest meals apart from the meals fed to the monks. Preferred guests always enjoyed the honor of eating at the abbot's table where choice meats and delicacies such as spiced figs and custard pies were served.

Payment for a night's accommodations was not required, but for the sake of the monastery it was expected. Too many unpaid nights created a financial hardship for the abbot, and it was his job to politely thank each departing guest for his stay to motivate him to reach into his pocket for some reasonable amount of money to cover meals and accommodations. Some, however, including occasional kings, were slow to reach for their silver coins as was the case of King John of England, according to Jocelin of Brakeland, a twelfth-century monk at the monastery of Bury St. Edmunds:

> He availed himself of the hospitality of St. Edmund, which was attended with enormous expense, and upon his departure bestowed nothing at all either of honor or profit upon the saint, save thirteen pence [pennies] sterling, which he offered at mass on the day of his departure.[31]

MEDICAL PRACTITIONERS

Maintaining a medical facility, which was called an infirmary, along with a medical practitioner called the infirmarian, was a job of great urgency required by the Rule of St. Benedict:

> Before and above all things, care must be taken of the sick, that they be served in very truth as Christ is served; because He hath said, 'I was sick and you visited Me.' Let

him [each monk] provide for the sick, the children, the guests, and the poor.[32]

Most of the great monasteries of medieval Europe that housed as many as two hundred monks at any time in addition to visiting travelers needed an infirmarian capable of treating the sick, the aged, and the terminally ill. Having a good infirmarian sometimes attracted elderly and terminally ill *conversi* who were sometimes willing to exchange their fortunes for reputable medical care.

Competent infirmarians understood many of the basic characteristics of a healthy body that aided their diagnosis of the sick. Most of the information they collected came from the use of their senses. Most tested a patient's temperature, for example, using his hand, knowing that an abnormally cold or hot touch indicated the presence of some illness. Some even understood the importance of immersing fevered patients in cold water to quickly drop their temperatures. Infirmarians also recognized the importance of a patient's skin color as an indicator of good health or illness and prescribed a variety of herbal remedies depending upon skin color. Smell and taste were commonly used to analyze a patient's blood, while smell and color of urine and feces provided rudimentary clues to potential internal ailments. Taking a patient's pulse to detect its strength, rather than rhythm or frequency, was believed to be an accurate indicator of health even though it was not known at the time that the heart circulated blood.

Cures for detected illnesses were generally not as scientific as the diagnosis. Infirmarians were limited to three known cures for most illnesses: dietary changes, application of herbal medicines, and bloodletting. Diet was known to play a role in health, and it was known that some foods were healthful and some were not. Onions and garlic, for example, were often prescribed for many illnesses, as were yams and some forms of mushrooms. As a way of improving the energy levels of the ill, infirmarians recommended eating increased amounts of red meat.

A variety of herbal medicines were considered "tried and true" remedies, the uses of which dated back to Greek and Roman times. All infirmarians were knowledgeable in the application of herbs, and they also knew how to grow them in special herb gardens.

When diet and herbs failed, infirmarians turned to bloodletting. They believed that many illnesses were the result of imbalances in the volume of blood: either too much or too little. Monks could not add blood to a patient, but they could remove some. To that end, bleeding was regularly recommended, and the preferred bodily location was always as close to the illness as possible. The most common method was to create a small incision in a vein and allowing some blood to drain. Another popular method was to apply leeches to the patient's skin until a few ounces of blood were sucked out.

ADMINISTERING THE MONASTERY

The parochial work of practicing medicine, feeding the poor, tending livestock, and working in the garden could not have taken place with such efficiency were the monasteries not carefully organized and administered. Not all monks followed the principle set out by St. Benedict of commitment to physical work. His sixth-century vision of monasteries offering monks relatively simple lives of prayer and work gradually evolved over many centuries into a fairly complex enterprise. As monasteries grew and expanded, they took on the appearance of small villages. They catered to the spiritual, intellectual, and everyday personal needs of the monks; provided a variety of alms to the poor; sheltered weary travelers; cared for the sick; and maintained the monastery grounds and buildings. To ensure smooth operations for the army of workers needed to make all of this possible, the task of administration became the most complex job within the monastery walls.

Coordinating the daily activities of one hundred monks or more while juggling the occasional need to work with

❧ MEDICAL GARDENS ❧

Herbs were known to cure many common illnesses, and monks were encouraged to experiment with them. A small portion of each vegetable garden was regularly dedicated to the cultivation of medical herbs. Each herb was believed to cure one or many illnesses.

Common treatments included pounding henbane, a plant causing a mild sedation, and hemlock, a poisonous plant, and laying the mixture on painful muscles; drinking a variety of common herbs to cure jaundice; and chewing laurel leaves, swallowing the juice, and laying the leaves on the navel to cure stomach cramps.

Some concoctions were complicated and required considerable work and patience to make. The following medieval prescription for lung ailments is provided by Susan Wallace in her article "Commonly Used Medical Plants," found on the website *Exploring the Middle Ages:*

"Take barley water which has been strained, raisins, violets, jujube, seed of melon and gourd, wheat starch, licorice, black plums, fennel root, parsley, wild celery, anise, caraway, and make thereof a syrup. That is to say, seep all these in water until the virtue of them be in the water. Then strain it and add sugar or honey. And then set it over the fire to steep softly. Then take the white of four eggs and beat them well and add them. And always skim it until it is clear. Then take it down and strain it clean so that no dregs remain therein. Put it in a closed vessel."

the local townspeople was the primary responsibility of the abbot. As a man with final authority over the entire monastery, he was constantly kept busy overseeing squabbles among the men, ensuring the observation of all rules, disciplining disobedient monks if necessary, receiving new monks into the order, procuring the food and materials needed for the successful running of the monastery, greeting visiting dignitaries, traveling to town to assist civic leaders, and traveling to Rome from time to time to visit the pope.

All of these administrative responsibilities tended to separate the abbot from the routine life of his monks. By the twelfth century, according to C.H. Lawrence, "It became the normal practice for the abbot to have his own house, with a hall, kitchen, and chapel, within the enclosure."[33] This turn of events meant that the responsibility for maintaining normal life and discipline in the cloister fell to his second in command, the prior. In the larger monasteries, there were two priors: one who oversaw all activities within the walls and one who tended to all matters relating to the outside world.

Beneath the abbot and priors, chain of command evolved that segmented each monastery. The cantor spent most of his day taking charge of and organizing all activities involving prayer, singing, and supplying materials for the hand copying of music and books. The sacrist cared for the preservation, clean-

Medieval monasteries were complex communities that needed to be carefully organized and governed.

ing, and display of all sacred relics such as ancient crosses, bones of saints, handcrafted mosaics, tapestries, and stained-glass windows. The almoner saw to the collection and supply of charitable food, clothing, and money to the poor, while the guest master was constantly running about trying to anticipate how many guests might be spending the night, getting rooms cleaned, and notifying the cellarer how many special meals would be needed that night. The cellarer, working primarily with young novitiates and even younger oblates, spent his day preparing hundreds of meals (in the larger monasteries) suitable to specific diets of both monks and visiting dignitaries.

Controlling chaos became the labor for these administrators. As more and more administrative jobs were added, each became increasingly focused and removed from the real duties of prayer and work as envisioned by St. Benedict.

The harder they worked to provide the greater community of monks with their opportunities for prayer and work, the further this select group of monks drifted from their essential vows.

This fact was not lost to some administrative monks. Although they recognized their administrative work was necessary, some monks nonetheless sought transfers from large monasteries to small ones where they could return to simple prayer and simple work.

Other administrative monks, however, saw opportunities to expand the role of work to include more than hard physical labor. This farsighted group saw opportunities for monks to specialize in work that could not be performed by the lay population. These monks focused their work on furthering the aims of scholarship and education that had first been developed by the Greeks and then by the Romans.

CHAPTER 4

SCHOLARS

Monks were among the literate segment of medieval society. Exempt from the daily tedium experienced by villagers plowing fields, milling flour, sewing clothes, fighting wars, or caring for families and children, monks had the freedom to learn how to read and write. Many monks made lifelong commitments to the preservation and advancement of scholarly work, which brought considerable distinction to the entire monastic movement throughout medieval Europe. Working under austere conditions, scholarly monks enjoyed passing part of their day reading Greek and Roman texts, hand copying manuscripts, writing theological treatises, learning about the natural world, and teaching.

From the beginning of the Middle Ages, a few monasteries became learning centers. Many maintained schools and libraries and were responsible for furthering the arts and sciences. Although monasteries were founded with the idea of withdrawal from secular life, they became a major force in the secular world of literature, philosophy, science, agriculture, and government. These monasteries were especially attractive to wealthy nobles; who sent their sons there along with sizeable financial contributions. These donations allowed the monks to purchase books, build libraries, fund master scholars, and pay for educational travel to foreign countries.

The most pressing work requiring the skills of scholar monks was the preservation of old, fragile Greek and Roman manuscripts that were crumbling and disappearing at an alarming rate. To address this desperate situation, monasteries began teaching scribes the art of hand copying the cracked, torn, and faded thoughts of the greatest Greek and Roman intellectuals.

SCRIBES

The Rule of St. Benedict encouraged monks to read books to educate themselves. Finding books to read during the early Middle Ages, however, was not an easy undertaking. Lacking paper, printing presses, and public libraries, only those with a great deal of money could afford to purchase their own books, each of which had to be

A page from a thirteenth-century manuscript shows a group of Franciscan monks discussing manuscripts. Monks were among the most dedicated scholars of medieval society.

copied by hand from another person's copy. Hand copying a book could take many months, depending upon the length of the book, and it cost a fortune.

The copying of books, technically called manuscripts—a word derived from the Latin compound *manu,* meaning "hand," and *script,* meaning "writing"— was a job perfectly suited for monks, who were required to spend part of their day performing work within the monastery. As the copying of manuscripts spread throughout Europe, monasteries earned a reputation as centers of learning and scholarship.

Thousands of old manuscripts had already been lost by the time monks began copying and preserving them because the material they were writ-

---

⚜ MEDIEVAL INSTRUCTIONS FOR PREPARING PARCHMENT ⚜

Preparing parchment in the larger monasteries kept many scribes busy. The process involved many highly specialized jobs. Preparing the thousands of animal skins used for the parchment varied a bit from place to place, but the following list describes the major steps:

- Skin a goat, lamb, or calf. (Sometimes even a pig, deer, or squirrel.)
- Wash the skin in clear, cold running water for twenty-four hours.
- Remove the hair of the skin by soaking the skins in wooden or stone vats in a solution of lime and water for three to ten days.
- Remove the wet, slippery skins and drape them hair-side out over a great curved wood surface, called a beam. Then stand behind the beam, lean forward over the top, and scrape away the hair with a long curved knife with a wooden handle at each end.
- Flip the skin over and scrape away the residue of clinging flesh. Be careful not to cut through the skin.
- Degrease the skin with a series of chalk applications to both sides of the wet skin. This repeated dusting with chalk leaches oils from the skin.
- If there are any small cuts in the skin, sew them up so they will not enlarge during the drying process.
- Stretch the skin taut on a frame until dry.
- When it is dry, scrape and shave the skin with fine pumice to smooth the skin. Fluffy little peelings will fall away that can be boiled to make glue.
- Cut the skin to the desired size.

ten on, such as papyrus, a form of paper made from fibers from the papyrus plant, and parchment, the dried and treated skins of goats and sheep, had disintegrated. Consequently, some of the greatest works by Greek writers of the fourth and fifth centuries B.C. such as Aristotle, Aeschylus, Thucydides, and Sophocles, had already disappeared, and medieval scholars were anxious to make copies of those that had survived.

Many monasteries contained a room called a scriptorium where monk copyists, called scribes, sat and worked. Each scriptorium had a director to oversee the selection of manuscripts to be copied and the quality of the final product. Because each manuscript was copied by hand, mistakes were easily made and each page required a careful proofreading. The scriptorium was furnished with specially constructed tables where scribes sat, either on a stool or on their knees to copy the works. Each table had a wooden holder for the page being copied, a sloping desk surface for the fresh page, and a small table for scribes' tools. Their assortment of tools included quills from swans, geese, or crows; ink pots; a small knife called a pen knife for sharpening their quills; and a compass used to regulate the spaces between letters, words, and lines.

Sitting at his table, each scribe generally received four sheets of parchment or papyrus at a time. He folded each piece in half and then into quarters, to

make sixteen pages. He affixed a mark on each page that identified him as the scribe, determined the correct spacing and the size of the letters, and dipped his quill in the ink pot. Slowly and meticulously he copied page after page. The tip of the quill gradually spread with use, requiring the scribe to sharpen the tip every eight or ten letters. If a mistake was discovered that could not be corrected—an egregious error—the sheet was destroyed and a new one issued.

Scribes had other commitments besides their work in the scriptorium, so often they completed only one lengthy book a year or three or four short ones. Some scribes developed excellent reputations throughout the literate segment of society that read and appreciated their work. Such monks enjoyed their reputation and strove to perfect their art. Others, however, often complained about their working conditions by leaving personal comments in the margins, known as marginalia, such as

"Only three fingers are writing, but the whole body is suffering," "Finally it is dinner time," "The scribe has a right to the best wine," "My parchment is the roughest in the world," and "I am not sure if the number [I am copying] is 1,000 or 10,000."[34]

As manuscripts gained in popularity, scribes added simple artistic decorations called illuminations. At first these colorful artistic touches were simple, but with time the decorations became increasingly elaborate and colorful. Eventually, an entirely different group of monks called illuminators specialized in applying the colorful ink.

ILLUMINATORS

A small number of special and very expensive manuscripts were chosen for decoration with colorful illuminations. These specially illuminated manuscripts had great value to collectors, who treasured them not so much as scholarly works but rather as works of art. Some of these rare manuscripts commanded high prices.

Monks began to produce illuminated manuscripts for generous monastery patrons and high-level church officials. Monks learned to create a wide range of decorative motifs, from the simple enlargement and coloring of the first letter of each chapter to placing decorative vines on the top of each page, to the far more elaborate full-page polychrome depictions of biblical scenes that even included thin leaves of gold.

When an illuminator received a completed page from a scribe, he saw blank spaces reserved for his artwork and received direction specifying the size and colors of ink to be used. The space on the parchment to be painted was initially given a fine rubbing with a pumice stone or finely powdered glass mixed in a piece of bread to create a smooth finish.

Following this final cleaning, one of two approaches was taken to accomplish the painting of the design. If a monastery did not have well-trained illuminators, then the pictures would be copied from books of designs that could be purchased. In such cases, the illuminator would actually trace a design from a design book. One technique for tracing, called "pouncing," required the illuminator to prick the outline of the original with a pin hundreds of times. The outline was then placed over the new page and dabbed with charcoal dust to create a dotted line that would then be covered with permanent black ink and filled in with colored ink. Favorite colors were vivid shades of green, red, blue, yellow, and lavender.

Well-trained illuminators worked freehand and were valued for their skills in creating unique designs. The first step required the blank space, which would receive the decoration, to be lightly crosshatched with light red ink to create small squares of equal size. Using the crosshatching as a guideline for accurate spacing, outlines were lightly sketched freehand in pencil or charcoal to ensure correct spacing and consistent shape before applying permanent ink. If errors were made, erasure was easily accomplished with a few light strokes of a pumice stone. These preliminary outlines were then copied over with black ink and the interiors filled in with colored ink, using either a quill or small brush.

The initial "O" from an Italian manuscript shows the intricate artwork illuminators created to decorate medieval manuscripts.

Occasionally, illuminators used gold leaf the thickness of tissue paper. To ensure good adhesion of the very thin leaves to the parchment, all gold work was done prior to the application of any ink. The key was to apply good-quality glue to the parchment first. Once dried, the gold was burnished with a smooth spoonlike tool to add luster, which when it caught the light, caused the gold to stand out dramatically from the rest of the page.

BINDERS

When all work on a manuscript was completed, different monks took responsibility for binding the pages together into a book. Many techniques

❧ INVENTORS OF LANGUAGE ❧

As Christianity spread to the outer borders of Europe following the collapse of the Roman Empire, translations of the Bible and other religious documents were provided in many obscure languages used by remote tribes. Since the only literate group was the monks, they sometimes first needed to develop an alphabet for people who did not have a written language.

Perhaps the most famous alphabet developed by Christian monks was the Cyrillic alphabet. It was developed by two brothers, Cyril and Methodius, who were missionaries to the Slavic people in the ninth century. The brothers became monks and were sent to Eastern Europe near the city of Constantinople, modern-day Istanbul. The language of church writings in the east was Greek, but Cyril believed that all people should learn to praise God in their own language, which he believed to be the only way they could understand and practice Christianity properly.

At that time, the Slavic peoples did not have an alphabet, so Cyril invented an alphabet especially for them that bore his name: Cyrillic. He principally used Greek letters, but he also used some Armenian and Hebrew letters, as well as some letters he invented for particular Slavic sounds. Examples of unusual letters unique to Cyrillic are: Д, Ж, Л, Ч, and Щ. The Cyrillic alphabet is still in use today in Russia, Bulgaria, Serbia, and among other Slavic peoples. When Cyril died in 869, Methodius translated the entire Bible into the Slavic language using his brother's alphabet.

were used, but the most common in monasteries was to sew the pages together in groups, called fascicles. The fascicles, between ten and fifteen pages, were then placed within a cover made of wood or heavy leather. The attachment of the covers was generally accomplished by pounding wood pegs through them and through the ends of the stitched fascicles.

All books kept within the library of a monastery were then taken to the library by the binders and placed on a shelf for permanent housing. One end of a heavy chain was screwed into the back cover and the other end screwed into the bookshelf. In this way, these valuable books did not disappear.

Scribes and illuminators became familiar with both Greek and Latin while copying manuscripts. Many monks recognized that the Greek language, in particular, was not only very complicated but it had changed in the past thousand years. For these reasons, learning Greek and establishing standards for the language became an important undertaking for some monks.

CURATORS OF THE GREEK LANGUAGE

Interest in ancient manuscripts went far beyond simply copying them. Some of the monks in the larger monasteries were scholars whose job was to study the ancient writings of great thinkers and philosophers. Favored writers were Greek philosophers such as Aristotle, Plato, Heraclitus, as well as the early Christians who wrote the New Testament in Greek. Studying the writings of these great minds assisted scholarly monks such as St. Thomas

A sixteenth-century Spanish painting depicts monks copying and studying ancient texts in the scriptorium of a monastery.

Aquinas and St. Francis of Assisi to formulate their own Christian writings that influenced intellectual trends in medieval Europe.

When these scholarly monks assembled to discuss early Greek writers, however, they found themselves disagreeing over what the Greek said. What they discovered was that each of them was reading the Greek in a different way because early Greek writers wrote their lines of text differently from the way medieval Europeans wrote their lines of text. The two differences causing them problems were that Greek sentences did not have spaces between the words and that Greek text was written alternately from left to right and from right to left. These two differences confused the monks and caused mistranslations.

The first problem that needed a solution was adding spaces between the words. Greek writers and their readers, who were perfectly comfortable with the language, could easily make sense of sentences without spaces, but monks translating thousand-year-old texts arguedwhereonewordendedandthenextbegan. To eliminate unnecessary confusion, monks discussed each Greek manuscript and agreed on spacing to assist future readers.

The second alteration corrected a form of Greek writing called boustrophedon, a word describing how oxen plow fields, first from left to right and then, as the oxen turn around, from right to left. Greek writers and readers understood that it was much faster to write and read in both directions rather than stop at the right edge of a page, move one's eyes to the left edge, and start all over again. Consequently, an ancient Greek sentence began in one direction but ended in the other. The solution to this problem was to instruct scribes that, when they copied the old Greek manuscripts, they should copy in only one direction on the new ones.

These two changes preserved and standardized Greek manuscripts so future generations could read and understand them. Monks began a valuable tradition of transcribing and, in the process, made valuable contributions to the language.

MEDICAL RESEARCHERS

The exploration of the human body fascinated a few medieval infirmarians, who preferred to expand their knowledge of medicine through research rather than by practicing it. One of the reasons monks lead the way in medical research was their access to Greek and Latin texts that were being copied by scribes. While copying many of the writings of early medical researchers such as the Greek physicians Hippocrates and Galen, monks discovered and read about dissections and descriptions of all of the major organs of the human body. As a result, some monasteries became the best early re-

❧ MEDIEVAL SHORTHAND ❧

One of the most important skills developed by monk copyists was a medieval form of shorthand. It was used to reduce the number of letters needed to convey ideas and information. Copyists were motivated to develop shorthand because of the high cost of parchment and papyrus, to achieve efficiencies in the labor of copying, and to reduce the size of books, which needed to be stored.

Over time, monks developed an elaborate system for abbreviating words and for replacing some commonly repeated phrases with symbols. These abbreviations were such an established part of transcribing and reading Latin for so long that the system was carried over wholesale into early printed books.

Forms of shorthand became so commonly used and copied that modern-day paleographers, who are scholars studying ancient writing, claim that they can date a manuscript based on the system of abbreviation alone. Paleo- graphers have amassed a dictionary of 14,000 distinctive shorthand marks. Some examples follow:

The ampersand (&), meaning "in addition to."

e.g., meaning "for example" from the longhand Latin "exempli gratia."

i.e., meaning "that is," from the longhand Latin "id est."

Mr., meaning "Mister."

W^m, meaning "William."

Sp, meaning "semper," Latin for "always."

7, meaning "perfectus," Latin for "done."

9 meant "com," and was combined with other words. When combined with "fort," for example, it made "9fort," meaning 'comfort'; "9plete" meant "complete."

search facilities. According to historian Andrew Dickson White,

The places where medicine, such as it thus became, could be applied, were at first mainly the infirmaries of various monasteries, especially the larger ones of the Benedictine order: these were frequently developed into hospitals. Many monks devoted themselves to such medical studies as were permitted, and sundry churchmen and laymen did much to secure and preserve copies of ancient medical treatises.[35]

These texts stimulated monks' interest in furthering medical research. The Church opposed the dissection of bodies to gain medical knowledge of anatomy, yet it permitted infirmarians to perform occasional postmortem examinations to determine cause of death. Monks learned basic lessons about anatomy by opening a dead person's abdominal cavity with butcher knives and removing and examining the organs. They inspected organs, looking for abnormal shapes, unusual smells, and odd coloration. One well-known medieval sketch dating to about 1300 shows a dissection being performed by an infirmarian holding a knife and assisted by a monk in the traditional habit. The dead person has a large incision in his abdomen, and around the body are drawn sketches of kidneys, intestines, a heart, and other organs.

Basic research was also carried out to learn how to set broken bones, suture deep wounds, remove urinary and bowel obstructions, and open blocked tracheas by cutting directly through the throat. The one piece of knowledge that monks worked to discover, with only minimal success, was the use of anesthesia. Many potions were known to medical men that were to be used during surgery. Some of the potions used to relieve pain or induce sleep were themselves potentially lethal. For example, one of these called for lettuce, gall from a castrated boar, opium, and hemlock juice; the hemlock juice could easily have killed the patient. The margin of safety between effective anesthesia and death was dangerously narrow.

Not all monks saw their work as providing research and scholarship. Some found outlets of expression in the visual arts, while others were inclined toward music. Fortunately for the general community of brethren, a handful of monks at most monasteries found artistic outlets that beautified the daily lives of all with art and music.

CHAPTER 5

ARTISTS AND MUSICIANS

As thousands of monasteries flourished across Europe over several centuries, many evolved to emphasize different traditions of work required of their monks. Some monasteries, for example, emphasized charitable works to assist the poor and sick, while others emphasized scholarly works to educate teachers and students. A few, most notably in Italy and France, encouraged their monks to work in the aesthetic disciplines of art and music. As a result of these artistic monks, one of the great legacies handed down from the medieval period was their rich tradition of art and music, which provided stepping stones for many early Renaissance artists and musicians.

In the sixth century, Pope Gregory the Great made a plea that scriptural scenes be depicted on the walls of churches for the benefit of the illiterate. Pictures of biblical scenes, the pope argued, could educate those who could not read about important Christian history and beliefs. Five hundred years later in 1025, at a meeting of Church leaders at Arras, France, the bishop made a similar plea for more forms of art in monasteries and churches noting, "It enables illiterate people to learn what books cannot teach them." [36]

Artists of the early Middle Ages were not famous masters. In fact, very little is known about most of them, yet according to one medieval historian writing for the website Beyond Books, "They were first and foremost monks and craftsmen whose work was valued simply not for its artistic rendering but for its spiritual provocation." [37]

The earliest and most prolific ecclesiastical art form that began cropping up in medieval European monasteries was mosaic.

This painting shows a group of men admiring frescoes painted on a church. Monks often used visual art to tell biblical stories to the largely illiterate population of the middle ages.

MOSAICS

Mosaic, the art form of depicting scenes in tiny colored stones, ceramics, gems, sea shells, and other hard materials, was the earliest art form known to have been executed by medieval monks. Mosaic scenes were created as visual reminders of biblical stories for monks as they moved from building to building within their monasteries. Although some abbots viewed colorful artistic depictions of biblical scenes a violation of St. Benedict's Rule that emphasized the importance of living simple and humble lives, most believed the richly colored mosaics glorified their religion.

Unlike the stories told by the fluid application of paint, mosaics told their stories with thousands, and sometimes tens of thousands, of colorful cubes no bigger than a fingernail called tesserae. Mosaics were placed on floors, walls, and even ceilings. Regardless of location, the process was the same: create the design, cut the pieces, and cement them in place.

When an abbot decided to add a mosaic, some monks committed their labor to creating it rather than tending the garden or cutting wood for the fire.

The creators of mosaics approached their work much like a painter; they decided on a theme, selected the location, sketched its design, and finally chose color schemes. The location was sanded smooth, patched if necessary, and thoroughly cleaned; then the design was drawn in charcoal. If changes were made, the charcoal was easily sanded off and the design redrawn.

The next task was making the tesserae. The most commonly used tesserae were painted ceramic tiles fired in very hot ovens called kilns. Only the largest monasteries could afford to build a kiln fired by wood or charcoal; the rest purchased their tiles. Before firing, the one-foot-square soft clay tiles were incised

By carefully arranging tiny colored tiles, medieval monks created beatiful works of art, like this sixth-century mosaic of an angel.

in a crosshatched pattern with a string or thin wire every quarter or half inch to create the small tesserae.

When the needed quantity and colors of tesserae were finished, the physically demanding job of setting them was often turned over to the oblates and novitiates under the supervision of the monk managing the project. This job was tricky because although the setters could look at the sketched outline on the wall or floor and see where the tesserae were to go and what color was to be used, the sketch had to be covered with an inch of wet sand and cement into which they would set the cubes. Since this application of sand and cement covered the outline, the monks who were the master setters laid down the wet substance only to small sections at a time. Occasionally, monks sketched part of the design on a piece of wood to be used as a reference they could look at after the cement covered the actual site.

The tesserae were then set, one at a time. The next day, when the cement had hardened, the final job of filling in the tiny gaps between the tesserae took place. Novitiates used their bare hands to spread a layer of very thin cement called grout over the entire picture and worked it down into the tiny spaces. Before it was allowed to harden, the surface of the entire mosaic was cleaned off with wet rags to remove the wet grout and reveal the surface of the thousands of colorful tesserae. This fi-

nal application of grout firmly set all the tesserae in place so the mosaic would adhere to a wall or be strong enough to withstand the feet of monks.

STAINED GLASS

The use of stained glass to decorate and beautify monasteries dates back to the late eleventh century. Monks recognized the value of placing windows in their chapels to admit light that illuminated notable biblical stories such as Christ's baptism, his crucifixion, and his resurrection within the windows themselves. The walls of monasteries were typically not very strong so windows were kept small. They were made large enough to admit enough light to illuminate a room during midday but not so large that the weight of the roof collapsed the windows.

As part of their requirement to perform *opus Dei,* some monks gravitated toward learning the craft of stained glass. In some of the larger monasteries such as Cluny, monks specialized in one of the three steps in its production: design, glazing, and assembly.

Design began with measuring the window opening and determining the subject of the window. Following that, the designer created a scale model of the window by gluing thin pieces of well-sanded wood planking together and cutting the planking to the actual size of the window. Next, he crosshatched the wood every inch with vertical and horizontal intersecting lines

☙ THE FIRST FAMOUS MONK PAINTER ❧

Monks created high-quality mosaics and stained glass throughout the the Middle Ages. Toward the end of that period, the first strokes of paint were being applied to canvas by the hands of creative monks. The first monk to produce the highest level of late-medieval art was Fra Angelico, a Dominican monk born in 1400 at the very end of the Middle Ages.

Fra Angelico began his life as an artist working as an illuminator in a monastery in Florence, Italy, when he was still an oblate teenager. But by the time he was twenty, he had wandered the streets of the city to study the paintings of the master painter Giotto di Bondoni that hung throughout Florence and other northern Italian cities. Giotto was not a monk, but his paintings glorified the life of Christ and other biblical figures.

All of Fra Angelico's paintings, on both wood panels and monastery walls, are considered by art historians remarkable for their cleanly defined lines, brilliant color, and spiritual expressiveness. His first painting was of the Virgin Mary, followed by paintings depicting St. Jerome, Mary and Jesus surrounded by twelve angels, and John the Baptist. As his fame spread, Fra Angelico supervised the fresco decorations of St. Mark's Monastery. Later in his life the Pope invited him to come to Rome to decorate the Cappella del Sacramento in the Vatican.

Fra Angelico focused exclusively on religious subjects while adopting the artistic innovations of his time. He was able to depict spatial depth that gave his works a three-dimensional quality that could not be achieved using mosaic or stained glass. He also influenced other painters with his sense of color and unity of composition.

---

either by using ink or by scoring the wood with a knife blade. This allowed him to space every figure perfectly and to keep all figures in correct proportion with all others. Once the surface was ready, he sketched the agreed-upon design over the crosshatching in charcoal. If he changed his mind, a light sanding removed the charcoal, but the crosshatching remained.

The design was then handed over to the glazer whose responsibility was to create the glass. Monks used one of two known methods to create stained glass: One group applied colored paint directly on transparent glass, while the other preferred to color the glass by applying various chemicals to the glass when it was molten hot. It was ultimately the latter technique that proved to be the best because the color penetrated the glass and was not subject to fading from exposure to the sun as was the case with applying paint.

A section of window from a thirteenth-century Cistercian monastery reveals how skillful monks were in creating stained glass.

As the glass melted, pigments were added to produce the desired color. Metallic oxides were added in small amounts to the clear glass to color it, and great skill was required to judge the correct amount to obtain the exact tone wanted. Cobalt oxide made blue glass, iron oxide made green, manganese oxide produced violet, flakes of gold or copper or selenium made red, coal and other carbon oxides produced amber, and black was produced from a combination of manganese, cobalt, and iron. According to art historian Caryl Coleman,

> The windows of the fourteenth century show a steady increase in knowledge of the art, more particularly in matters of drawing and harmonious use of color. The later advance was brought about by the discovery of the yellow stain, which placed in the artists' hands produced not only various shades of yellow, but also a color with which they could warm their white glass.[38]

Monks working with molten hot glass used furnaces heated with wood or charcoal that could produce the 650-degree-Fahrenheit temperatures required to melt glass. They achieved these temperatures by forcing air into the heated furnace with large bellows.

When the glass reached the desired color, it was poured into square forms on large flat, smooth stones until it cooled and hardened. At this point, the monks involved in assembly gathered the glass and cut it to the shapes specified on the wood model. Cutting was done by using an iron cutting tool that had been heated red-hot, and the glass was then trimmed with a second hot iron called a grozing iron. When all of the pieces were cut, they were assembled on the wood planks for a final check for accuracy. When the designing monk was satisfied, he ordered a half-inch seam of molten lead poured between each piece to hold them in place. When the lead hardened, the entire work was set into a frame and placed in the wall.

Mosaics and stained glass were not the only artistic visual representations intended to glorify the religious beliefs and traditions of the Church. A third, and perhaps the grandest, artistic statement for the monasteries was the architecture of their chapels.

ARCHITECTURE

Designing chapels was a far more complicated and challenging undertaking than creating mosaics and stained glass. Generally, architects studied for many years before attempting structures as complicated as chapels, and for that reason, most were members of secular society. In spite of its many

---

⚜ STAINED GLASS AND ARCHITECTURE ⚜

The introduction of stained glass greatly influenced and changed medieval architecture. The initial introduction of stained-glass windows during the twelfth century was considered a miraculous discovery. For the first time ever, large structures such as chapels and cathedrals could be illuminated during the day by sunlight, an experience so extraordinary that many people of the time considered it the leading discovery of its time.

As more and more windows were added to the walls of chapels, the walls became weaker because walls with glass were not as strong as those made of solid stone. Eventually, architects added too many windows to admit more and more light and the walls buckled under the tremendous weight of the roof and collapsed, killing many people.

Such catastrophes motivated architects to solve the problem of increasing the strength of walls while continuing to increase the size and number of windows. The best-known and most noticeable solution was the invention of massive supports called flying buttresses. These flying buttresses, made of brick and stone, were built outside the chapel wall as freestanding pilings with arching horizontal supports attached to the main walls.

Flying buttresses, stabilizing the walls, prevented them from collapsing under the weight of the roof. By employing these clever supports, architects could continue to add more stained glass, to the delight of those inside the chapels, without fear of collapsing walls and roofs.

complications, a few monks established excellent reputations as architects.

One of the most respected architects was Abbot Suger of the Monastery of Saint-Denis in France, who designed a chapel that was completed in 1144 along with several of the smaller buildings. Suger drafted the precise height, length, and width of foundations, rooms, and staircases on parchment. Additional sheets of parchment detailed such things as roof design, sculptural details, and the placement of doors and stained-glass windows. Because the plans were "one of a kind" and expensive to produce, they were carefully guarded. When the plans were no longer needed, the skins were scraped clean and reused. Over time, the parchment either became dry and brittle or eventually deteriorated.

One of the advantages of having a monk as the architect was that he was able to design a chapel that reflected the spiritual tradition of the church and would be of a size suitable to the monastery. Most contemporary art historians believe that Suger's architectural objective, which set him apart from secular architects, was to glorify Jesus. The basic interior design of the chapel, for example, resembled a cross, and it was purposely chosen to remind everyone entering of the cross on which Jesus was crucified. Suger also had Jesus in mind, as he recorded in his diary, when he designed the entry doors:

The main doors Bronze casters having been summoned and sculptors chosen, we set up the Main doors on which are represented the Passion of the Savior and His Resurrection, or rather Ascension, with great cost and much expenditure for their gilding as was fitting for the noble porch. [39]

Suger also designed the chapel with a revolutionary spire, the tallest anywhere in France at that time. He admittedly did so to compete with other great chapels being built throughout Europe and because he wanted to make the symbolic statement that his chapel was reaching higher and closer to Jesus. Suger also pioneered the design of stone buttresses that prevented walls from collapsing and the design of vaults inside the chapel that assisted the walls in supporting the ceiling. In keeping with his architectural theme of glorifying Jesus, he designed small decorative details depicting the life of Jesus in the vaults and buttresses. The architectural theme of glorifying Christ extended to other creative endeavors as well.

MUSIC

Music, much like visual monastic art, was found in all monasteries. And much like the visual arts, it was composed to glorify major biblical figures, events, and traditions. The need for music stemmed from the belief that singing was a holy way to pray and

A medieval fresco shows a monk playing a guitar-like instrument called a lute. Music was an important component of monastic life.

from the need for a variety of musical choices for prayers performed many times each day. To accommodate the monks' needs for a variety of music, the cantor of each monastery was kept busy composing new pieces.

Unfortunately, however, very few written medieval compositions have survived. When cantors composed them, often one or more each week, they were intended to be used for no more than a month or so. As a result, only a few were actually written on parchment with the intention of using them for years. For the vast majority of songs, the words were memorized, writ-

ten on wood tablets and later erased, or the cantor would first sing each line and the choir of monks would simply repeat what he sang. Nonetheless, musicologists are able to trace the development of various musical styles that cantors developed.

Liturgical chants, songs written for specific uses in various church services, met the requirement of all chants, a melody executed by the human voice only. Cantors wrote what were referred to as plain chants that were sung in monotone. Since such plain songs could rapidly become boring, cantors alternated between the bass voices of the monks and the alto voices of the young oblates to create variety.

By the end of the Middle Ages, a few of the more experimental cantors began to introduce the use of simple stringed instruments, principally the lyre and a miniature handheld harp. The use of these instruments in monastic settings was slow to gain acceptance even though their use was an immediate hit among the villagers and townspeople who heard them.

GREGORIAN CHANTS

Not all monks responsible for composing new songs each week were permitted the use of musical instruments. For these unfortunate composers, some other approach to reducing the monotony of all male singers was pursued. The primary complaint was that of the boring sound of monotone songs. To provide variety, a few cantors took the lead experimenting with variations on chants.

♪ MUSICAL NOTATION ♫

Prior to the invention of musical notation, no one knew how to record music on paper or parchment. The man who invented written musical notation in the eleventh century was the monk Guido d'Arezzo. Guido served as a Benedictine monk in France until traveling to work for Bishop Theobald in Arezzo, Italy, where he lived for several years. Although Guido was not a composer, he is revered by musicians because his contributions as an early music theorist made it possible for early composers to begin recording their work on manuscripts.

About 1025, Guido created a system of musical notation using a four-line staff that has evolved into the system we use today. The importance of this work is enormous. Before Guido's invention of musical notation, every singer had to memorize the entire chant repertoire. Those singers then went on to teach the

next generation. Small errors in memory or differences of taste caused the chants to change over the years, and no two singers would learn a chant precisely the same way. Notation made it possible to record a chant in a definitive form.

Guido also created the system of solemnization, more commonly known as the use of the syllables *doe, re, mi, fa, so,* and *la.* Guido discovered that using syllables to teach chants made it possible for his singers to learn new chants more quickly. He even created a method to teach the syllables by pointing to sections of his hand. The "Guidonian Hand" has been immortalized in numerous illustrations and was used widely as a teaching tool. Guido's innovative teaching methods even garnered attention from the papacy in Rome where he gave a demonstration of his teaching techniques to Pope John XIX in 1028.

Sometime between the late ninth and early tenth centuries in France, monks experimented with simple rhythms to give chants some variation. They called these new chants Gregorian chants, named after the sixth-century Pope Gregory. The most significant characteristic of these chants was their highly unorthodox rhythms. Without musical instruments to help maintain rhythm, and without any way to write music that could regulate duration of notes, cantors needed to find some other way to ensure that a group of singers could sing the same song, start and end at the same time, and keep pace with each other.

The unusual quality of Gregorian chants was their fluctuating movement, which is often described as being like a tide that rises and falls yet is different with each tide. Sometimes it can be quick, while at other times it is slow. And also like a tide, some chants were very quiet while others could be loud and forceful. The key to the chant is a constant smooth rise and then a smooth fall of volume and speed. They can create a trancelike quality.

To assist monks in knowing when their voices should rise or fall, and how quickly, cantors included simple accent marks in chant books. The general rule was that volume was built up gradually towards the accent and then decreased afterward. This gradual buildup followed by its decrease created a sound echoing throughout the chapel that monks and abbots appreciated for its simplicity. Singers gradually learned the chants' melodies by heart, permitting all to sing in perfect time and rhythm.

Most monks did not possess the creativity to contribute art forms and music. And many others realized that they could not spiritually thrive within the confining walls of their monastery. Fortunately for these monks, some monasteries allowed them to venture beyond the monastery walls to work.

CHAPTER 6

TRAVELING MONKS

Not all monks lived and worked secluded lives behind monastery walls. Although all were principally concerned with spiritual matters far removed from the events of the secular world, at times some felt it necessary to move out from the monastery into the towns, villages, and byways of Europe. These traveling monks broke from one of the most basic principles of monasticism when they chose to abandon the isolation and confinement of the monastery to oversee the spiritual needs of the common people where those people lived.

BEGGING MONKS

From as far back as the late Roman Empire, some monks eschewed the static communal life in monasteries in favor of lives spent roaming from town to town. Drawn to a nomadic life by biblical references to men who begged for their sustenance, some medieval monks believed that following their examples was one way to gain salvation for all of humanity. The one example most often cited was the life of Jesus because according to biblical tradition, he owned nothing, had no home, and depended upon the good will of his followers.

During the late twelfth century, begging monks were called mendicants, a word derived from the Latin word meaning "openhanded." Roaming from town to town, monks stopped and sat at prominent places on roads and opened their hands hoping for a handout. Some sat with open hands begging for coins, but most placed a small wooden bowl in front of them and prayed while begging for food. Passersby during times of poverty and social upheaval had little to contribute, but many believed that by contributing some morsel to the bowl, they might receive a blessing from the monk that would increase their possibility of going to heaven when they died. In exchange for food and clothing, some monks agreed to listen to people's personal problems and give advice while others made promises to pray for the release of souls of dead relatives who might not have gone to heaven.

As part of their tradition of begging, mendicants begged for shelter in strangers' homes. During cold nights, mendicants often exchanged an evening of prayer and spiritual conversation and occasionally listened to confessions for a dry place to sleep. In addition, literate monks were often willing to teach children to read Latin scripture.

At daybreak, monks departed once again for the open road. If traffic was light, mendicants wandered into towns and went from food shop to food shop looking for a few leftover scraps. One moral aspect of their work, however, was certain: None was to have more than was necessary for the moment. This sentiment was expressed by one French monk, Waldes, who proclaimed in 1181, ". . . nor will we accept gold or silver, or anything from anyone, except only food and clothing for the day."[40]

A group of Franciscan monks visits the pope in this fifteenth-century painting. Monks occasionally made such visits to solicit donations for their order.

Within two hundred years, an estimated ten thousand mendicant monks spread out across Europe. Major roads occasionally became cluttered with monks praying and begging for food. Shop owners occasionally accused a few of theft, and travelers experienced what some viewed as harassment for food. Some church and civic leaders complained that too many monks were simply lazy and did not want to work as monks living in monasteries tending their gardens, raising livestock, and copying books. The thirteenth-century writer and scholar Salimbene, sternly warned about mendicants, "They wish to live on the charity of the Christian people, although they do nothing for it, they hear no confessions, they do not preach, nor do they give edification."[41]

Salimbene was certainly correct on the last of these charges. Mendicants traveling the roads, rarely staying long in any one place, did not have the depth of understanding to meet the spiritual or intellectual needs of the educated secular people. To rectify this shortcoming, a small number to monks set out to learn and teach.

TRAVELING TO LEARN AND TEACH

Sophisticated townspeople, especially those living in cultural centers such as Paris, Bruges, Cologne, Athens, London, and Florence were often interested in far more than prayer and confession in exchange for food and clothing.

To meet the religious and intellectual needs of urbane people, some traveling monks added scholarship and teaching to their list of monastic responsibilities.

Individual monks who desired to deepen their knowledge of the church, its history, and other academic disciplines departed remote monasteries and flocked to newly established universities throughout Europe. Around 900, a monk by the name of Richer of Rheims wrote a history of France. In it he told of his journey from his monastery in Rheims to attend school in Chartres in hopes of studying under the well-known scholar Heribrand. As Richer indicates, noted scholars were often capable of attracting students and teaching many different academic disciplines:

Then I diligently began the study of the *Aphorisms of Hippocrates* with Heribrand, a highly cultured and scholarly man. I later learned the ordinary symptoms of diseases and picked up a surface knowledge of ailments. This was not enough to satisfy my desires. I begged him to continue to guide my studies on a deeper level, for he was an expert in his art and in pharmaceutics, botany and surgery.[42]

The collective goal of chosen monks was to study the subjects of logic, rhetoric, debate, Latin composition, and theology with leading scholars. Other subjects, however, such as art and the

Saint Augustine (with book in lap) presents his book of rules to his followers. Some monks left the confines of their monasteries to teach others and to study in Europe's new universities.

philosophy of Aristotle were considered to be the study of heathens, and monks were admonished to stay away.

In keeping with their vows of poverty, monks were provided with housing in churches or small monasteries near their universities during their seven years of formal education. Universities did not have a central campus, so monks needed to hurry across town to find their classes, most of which met daily. Classroom instruction, always conducted in Latin, usually began with a lecture given by the professor, which might be followed by questions from students. Some instructors preferred to employ a method of investigation called the Socratic dialogue, which drew students deeper into a subject by asking students probing questions about their

KNIGHTS OF TEMPLAR PUNISHMENT FOR INFRACTIONS

Every monastic order had strict rules and regulations, and the Knights Templar was no exception. When some infraction of the Rule occurred, the commander would call the monk brethren to hear the charges against an offender, and if the accused brother confessed his guilt, he was asked to leave the room. At this time the commander would seek the advice of the brethren on what penalty to apply. If the infraction was minor or if he was found to be innocent, then no penance would be given. If, however, he was guilty of a major infraction of the Rule, then the General Chapter would later try him.

Expulsion was the highest punishment a Templar Knight could face. Below is a list of the infractions that could trigger an expulsion taken from "Templar Punishment," at www. templarhistory.com:

- Murdering a Christian.
- Divulging the meetings of the Knights Templar.
- Committing acts of sodomy.
- Committing an act of heresy or denouncing the Christian faith.
- Conspiring or making false charges against a fellow Knight.
- Leaving the Temple house for more than two days without permission.
- Fleeing the enemy during battle.

Lesser infractions triggered lesser punishments. Minor infractions could cause loss of rank, separation from fellow monks, the embarrassment of eating off the floor, or being forced to perform a variety of menial tasks. These lesser punishments were imposed for infractions of the code of conduct such as:

- Fighting with another knight.
- Murdering a slave.
- Killing a pack animal or losing their horse due to their own neglect.
- Telling lies.
- Injuring any Christian person out of anger.
- Having sex with a woman.
- Throwing their Templar coat to the ground in anger.

statements and questions rather than simply answering them.

Although they were away from home, this was one of the few jobs away from their monasteries in which monks did

not need to beg for meals. Nonetheless, their standard of living was barely at the subsistence level. Although monks were absent from the many restrictions of a monastery, abbots warned them to continue the same modest lives in school that would be expected of them at their monasteries:

> While at university, enter and depart humbly, modestly, and devoutly. Let conversation be quiet and pleasing to God. Let no one make murmurs, babblings, scoffing, or indiscreet noises. We command all scholars that they shall always have, faithfully keep, and observe unity among themselves, with peace and concord and brotherly love. [43]

MISSIONARY MONKS

Recruiting and converting non-Christians to Christianity was another monastic responsibility that required some monks to travel. In keeping with the many traditions within the brotherhood of monks that emulated the work of Christ, the most effective and spiritually correct way to convert people was to go out and find them in the communities where they lived.

During the early Middle Ages, when most of the European population knew little if anything about Christianity, early church leaders such as Pope Gregory perceived the need to send monks out into small towns and villages far from Rome to spread the word. Gregory was especially keen to see monks travel to distant lands such as England and Scandinavia. The eighth-century church historian known as the Venerable Bede writes about Pope Gregory:

> Gregory, prompted by divine inspiration, sent a servant of God named Augustine and several more God-fearing monks with him to preach the word of God to the English race. [44]

Taking nothing more than their habits, Bibles, and wooden begging bowls, monks went forth as missionaries to convert as many people as possible. They went alone or sometimes in groups begging for food, clothing, and shelter as they wandered Europe's dirt roads, proselytizing. English historian David Ross comments,

> The monks of the 7th and 8th centuries were not confined to a closed monastic community, but carried the responsibility of traveling, usually on foot, throughout the surrounding countryside to preach and convert in the villages. [45]

Their task was to encourage non-Christians to convert to Christianity so their souls might go to heaven. Carrying their Bibles and rosaries, they spoke with whoever would listen about the life of Jesus and why his death on the cross was significant to Christians.

Working in foreign lands far from monasteries could be dangerous. Not everyone accepted what the missionary monks had to say. Many older religious doctrines existed in Europe long before Christianity and some of their adherents opposed the monks' teachings. Verbal dueling in towns and village squares sometimes escalated to verbal abuse and even physical violence. Disturbing biblical stories discussing the sacrament of communion caused much commotion and accusations because many thought it advocated cannibalism. More than one monk was beaten and thrown out of town for their attempts to convert the local population.

PILGRIM MONKS

An unusual form of devotion to the spirit of Christianity chosen by a small

Pilgrims on horseback pass a walled city on their way to a religious shrine. Some monks embarked on pilgrimages to distant lands in search of holy relics.

❧ FALSE PILGRIMAGES ❧

Not everyone was impressed by monks suffering as they walked and crawled from holy shrine to holy shrine. Seeing hundreds of monks begging as they traveled the roads of Europe and the Holy Land led many to question whether their motives were genuinely focused on moral prayer or if they were simply trying to get free food and free places to sleep. One such twelfth-century skeptic, quoted in Peter Speed's book Those Who Prayed, *made this observation about what he termed useless pilgrimages by monks:*

What is one supposed to think about pilgrimages by monks? Certainly they might redeem their own errors in performing penances more easily and fulfilling them in their own churches through the remedy of a more strict life. For it might be better to fulfill a work that is owed and to do even more to perform the penance that is taken up than by abandoning one office to wander about on a dubious pilgrimage.

Other thinkers saw pilgrimages by monks in different but equally critical ways. One church leader, the fifth-century spiritual leader, intellect, and writer St. Augustine, is quoted in Daniel Caner's book Wandering, Begging Monks *as cautioning pilgrim monks collectively,* "You ought not to be seeking an easy meal in idle travels, but that you ought to be seeking the kingdom of God through the straight and narrow life of this monastic profession."

number of medieval monks involved a painful tramping across Europe and the Middle East in imitation of Christ's wandering as a young man. Such travels, called pilgrimages, involved departing from monasteries on foot to visit holy relics at various cities throughout Europe and the Holy Land. Cities containing important shrines included Jerusalem; Constantinople (modern-day Istanbul, Turkey); Canterbury, England; Rome, Italy; and Compostela, Spain.

Holy relics were religious shrines containing sacred Christian objects such as the bones of saints, pieces of the cross on which Christ was cruci-

fied, and a variety of other artifacts once owned or used by biblical figures. Monks who traveled to shrines were known as pilgrims. They were motivated to make pilgrimages for the spiritual experience of seeing and touching well-known Christian relics in the belief that such devotion would please God and would increase the number of souls admitted to heaven. They further believed that touching a saint's relic was the same as touching the saint, who, in turn would intercede with God on behalf of the monk.

In keeping with the tradition of asceticism, the perfect pilgrimage for a monk involved suffering along the route. The attraction to such misery was the notion that the more one suffered, the more genuine was the commitment to venerate God. Monks were known to inflict maximum pain on pilgrimages. Some traveled part of each day on their knees, some bound their legs in chains, while others dragged a heavy stone harnessed to their backs. Stopping each night for lodging, monks on pilgrimages copied begging monks by setting out their wooden bowls and begging food from more affluent pilgrims who were willing to contribute to them in the belief that such acts of generosity would please God.

A few monks made pilgrimages one of their primary jobs, second only to prayer. Such men felt that suffering as they trekked across the landscape was their true calling as monks. According to historian Jean Décarreaux, one such well-known eighth-century English monk, St. Benedict Biscop, was "one of the most famous foot-pilgrims of the day, making no fewer than five journeys to Rome." [46]

WARRIOR MONKS

Of the many manifestations of traveling monks, none seemed more paradoxical than traveling off to war. All monks swore to obey many oaths and vows committing them to contemplative lives for the spiritual well-being of themselves and their followers, but killing was not included

in any of these oaths. Working in many ways to help others on rare occasions meant taking up arms in defense of the church. The end of the eleventh century ushered in one such occasion known as the Crusades, a four-hundred-year period of sporadic fighting between Christian and Muslim soldiers over control of land in the Middle East.

Beginning in 1095, Pope Urban II sent out a call to arms that even moved some monks to depart their monasteries to travel to the Holy Land to fight. In the belief that it was their spiritual obligation to defend lands where Jesus once lived, taught his followers, and died, some monks were willing to exchange their habits for full suits of armor. From their point of view, taking up arms in defense of Christianity was merely one of many tasks required of monks.

As more and more monks took up arms, they formed their own religious order called the Knights Templar. According to historian Robert Beecham,

> The Knights Templar was a monastic military order formed at the end of the First Crusade with the mandate of protecting Christian pilgrims on route to the Holy Land. Never before had a group of secular knights banded together and taken the monastic vows. In this sense they were the first of the Warrior Monks. [47]

Initially these warrior monks were known as the "Poor Knights" because of their vows of poverty and their oath to protect pilgrims going to the Holy Land. As the wars raged on generation after generation, however, they directly entered the bloody fray against Muslim armies. Monks trained with swords, bows and arrows, and on horseback. Their skill on the battlefields became legendary, and by the third Crusade, they acquired the reputation as ferocious soldiers. In keeping with their monastic traditions, the members of the Knights Templar held to the belief that death on the battlefield would be

Knights of the Muslim army ride into battle during the third crusade. Monks comprised some of the fiercest soldiers who fought against the Muslim armies.

received by God as a sign of devotion. Bernard of Clairvaux, the twelfth-century abbot of the monastery in Clairvaux, France, supported this view in his book *In Praise of the New Chivalry,* in which he praises the warrior monks:

> Go forward, therefore, in confidence, O knights, and with dauntless spirit drive out the enemies of the cross of Christ. Be certain that neither death nor life can divorce you from the love of God. With what happiness they die, martyrs in the battle! Rejoice brave athlete, if you live in and conquer in the Lord. But exalt and glory the more, if you should die and be joined to the lord. [48]

The choice to perform *opus Dei* within monastery walls or on the road seemed to meet the work interest of some monks but not quite all of them. A small number tenaciously clung to the belief that the best way to perform their *opus Dei* was to eschew all social contact in favor of a hermit's life, which focused exclusively on prayer and severe asceticism.

CHAPTER 7

HERMIT MONKS

Throughout the Middle Ages, there was always a group of monks who believed that the end of the world was near. Preparing for what they hoped would be everyone's imminent spiritual journey to heaven, they chose to immerse themselves in prayer. Such immersion meant eschewing all social contact with other people to pursue a strict life of asceticism—even a more extreme form than could be found in monasteries.

Such monks were called hermits, from the Greek word *eremite* meaning "desert" because many of them lived in very dry geographic environments. The meaning of the word *eremite,* or "hermit" in English, evolved over time from a person living alone in the desert to any person living an ascetic life alone in prayer and spiritual contemplation.

WORK ETHIC OF EXTREME ASCETICISM

The work ethic of hermit monks, the principles they followed to perform their work, was to pray not only in complete isolation but also under the harshest conditions possible. It was their opinion that the more they suffered while at prayer, the closer they would come to achieving an understanding of God and the more God would recognize the sincerity of their prayers. Hermit monks became the heroes of some people because they were seen much like Jesus himself to sacrifice their lives for sinners.

The earliest and most well-known hermit monk, St. Anthony, who lived during the fourth century, set himself apart from his fellow monks by his unusually harsh existence. He was said to have lived a life of such severe deprivation that his biographer, Athanasius of Alexandria, wrote of him,

> He kept vigil to such an extent that he often continued the whole night without sleep; and this not once but often, to the marvel of others. He ate once a day, after

A crumbling fourteenth-century fresco shows two hermit monks outside of their cave dwelling.

sunset, sometimes once in two days, and often even in [once in] four. His food was bread and salt, his drink, water only. Of meat and wine it is superfluous even to speak, since no such thing was found with the other earnest men. A grass mat served him to sleep upon, but for the most part he lay upon the bare ground. He would not anoint himself with oil [skin moisteners], saying it behooved young men to be earnest in training and not to seek what would enervate the body. [49]

Without any rules for communal living such as those found in monasteries, hermits were free to conduct their prayer as they wished. Some became so committed to prayer and to asceticism that they intentionally neglected their bodies. One such hermit was described by a medieval writer who said of him,

> He was forever fasting, and he had a garment [an animal skin] of hair on the inside while the outside was skin, which he kept until his end. And he neither bathed his body with water to free himself from filth, nor did he ever wash his feet. [50]

Such descriptions as these and others prompted the eighteenth-century historian Edward Gibbon to comment:

> It was the practice of the hermit monks neither to cut or shave their hair; they wrapped their heads in a cowl, to escape the sight of profane objects; their legs and feet were naked, except in the extreme cold of winter; and their slow and feeble steps were supported by a long staff. The aspect of a genuine hermit was horrid and disgusting; every sensation that is offensive to man was thought acceptable to

God; and the angelic rule of Tabenne [a hermit enclave] condemned the salutary custom of bathing the limbs in water, and of anointing them with oil. [51]

DESERT DWELLERS

Unlike monks living in monasteries or monks traveling throughout Europe, the work of a hermit was not defined by providing for the well-being of others or any *opus Dei*. Quiet prayer and contemplation was their path to heaven. The attraction to deserted areas was in part motivated by biblical tradition and in part by each monk's pursuit of uninterrupted prayer. They equated living near other people and normal conversation as impediments to their work of prayer.

To this end, many monks initially set out into the deserts and other remote areas in Europe beginning at the start of the sixth century, and within two hundred years, thousands were dwelling in remote areas. This call to isolated prayer continued throughout the Middle Ages.

Hermits often practiced their prayer and withdrawal from the world in an eccentric manner. Emulating the lives of many biblical figures, dwelling in desert regions, or at least very remote areas far from towns and people, made for the difficult life they sought for their primary job of prayer. Most hermits lived in crude caves or dugout burrows in the sand or dirt to avoid the heat of day and the cold of night. Old manuscripts provide drawings of monks huddled inside of burrows and caverns where they prayed and slept. Within the burrow, monks slept on the bare ground, sitting or reclining against a dirt wall. Roots, smooth stones, or mats woven from reeds served as pillows. One such desert dweller by the name of St. Sabinus prided himself on sitting motionless in his burrow where, according to historian Jacques LaCarrière, "He ate neither bread nor anything that is

A sixteenth-century fresco depicts an order of hermit monks gathered in prayer near their caves outside the city.

❧ THE ADULATION OF THE XENITEIA ❧

Many medieval Europeans were very much impressed with hermit monks who were able to perfect the spiritual asceticism of xeniteia, the endless wandering from place to place, typically in a foreign land. Such monks were demonstrating, in their unique way, that they could overcome any of life's stresses merely by trusting in their ability to continually be on the move. To most of the peasant population that suffered from the ravages of acute poverty, disease, and the oppression of the wealthy nobility, such monks were perceived as heroes. Historian Daniel Caner quotes one medieval source in his book Wandering, Begging Monks *as saying,*

There is no care for food or concern for clothing. If one of them lacks his basic necessities, he does not turn to a city, village, or family member to get what he needs, for his will by itself suffices.

When he raises his hands and utters words of thanksgiving to God, all these things are instantly provided for him.

Another of the attractions of the Xeniteia for European peasants was what appeared to be lives free of care and worry. This perception was common to many, as Caner reports, quoting one sixth-century writer, Abba Bessarion:

No concern for a dwelling troubles them, nor did any desire for a particular place ever control them, nor did the enjoyment of delights, possessions of houses, or reading of books. Instead, they seem completely detached from all passions of the body, being nourished on the hope of things to come. They live happily along the desert's edge like vagabonds.

eaten with bread, living entirely on flour which he left soaking in water for a month so that it would smell bad and taste worse."[52]

As some remote areas attracted more and more hermits, some felt the need to find even more isolated places to pray. Some, called the Grazers, were monks who lived in the wilds without permanent residence. Foraging in the woods and meadows like wild animals, they ate wild herbs that they snatched up in their teeth like animals. Still another group, called Xeniteia, from the

Greek word for "foreigner," lived lives constantly on the move from place to place—each resigned to live alone in a land not his own.

Yet at the same time, many other hermits believed that they needed to expand their duties beyond isolated prayer to include teaching by example. Perceiving themselves as beacons of light for the value of asceticism, these hermit monks sought to make public examples of their prayer and asceticism. To make their lives more widely known to others, they found highly unusual places to perform their prayer so others could observe and learn from them.

DENDRITES AND STYLITES

Beginning in the sixth century, a few Greek hermits, who were determined to take literally Christ's instruction to behave like the birds of the air, decided to live in trees. This unusual group, called Dendrites from the Greek word for "tree," actually built nests for themselves in the branches of large trees or crawled into hollowed-out tree

❧ METEORA AND STYLITE MONKS ❧

One of the most prominent geographical locations that attracted scores of Stylite hermits was a location in central Greece called Meteora. Thousands of years ago seismic pressure forced dozens of stone pinnacles to rise a thousand feet above the valley below. When this location was discovered by Stylites, they quickly scrambled to the tops of several peaks to escape the villagers living below.

By the eighth century, Meteora, a Greek word meaning "hovering in air," had become one of Europe's most spectacular sacred sites. The only access to the tops of the many peaks was by scaling the vertical bases. Hermit monks hauled food up with them so they would not need to make the climb more than once a week. The strenuous climb had the value, however, of deterring bothersome curiosity seekers.

By the eleventh century, many individual Stylites living exposed to the elements on top of the pinnacles and in small caves began to pool their energy to build simple shelters on the tops of several pinnacles. As they hauled wood and other building materials to the tops,

basic shelters went up. When communities began to pray and live together, more monks joined the dozen or so communities and the need to expand grew. Within another hundred years, elaborate systems of winches and pulleys attached to baskets were made to lift permanent building materials such as brick and concrete to the peaks. The baskets made the trip up and down much easier for the monks as well.

Still lacking easy access, the simple structures evolved into more complex monasteries, and they eventually attracted scholars and artists. Mosaic works were created that attracted visitors from throughout Europe, and their libraries of ancient Greek manuscripts were ranked among the very best. Yet, the monks were always easily able to control visitors because, to get to the tops, they had to request permission. This was done by finding a basket suspended by a rope and pulling on it, which rang a bell high up in the monastery. If the monks wished to admit the visitor, they signaled to get into the basket and a team of monks winched the visitor to the top.

In this sixth-century mosaic, a Stylite perches on a pillar. Some monks believed that praying atop such pillars brought them closer to God.

trunks. Others of this group, who preferred to live in caves, suspended themselves in iron cages to seem to live like birds.

A second group, also responding to a Bible passage, determined to live atop tall pillars of rock because of a passage that recommends that people live as close to God as possible. Thinking this meant literally to live as close to heaven as possible, these hermits, called Stylites from the Greek word for "pillar," either built pillars or inhabited natural ones found in rocky mountains.

Both Dendrites and Stylites used their elevated positions for prayer and for teaching. What they discovered was that they developed reputations as holy thinkers that attracted people to seek them out, observe them, and to occasionally seek advice. The most famous Dendrite was David of Thessalonica,

Greece, whose long ascetic career included three years in an almond tree, from which he prayed and addressed followers who clustered at the base of his tree.

The most famous Stylite was the monk Simon the Elder. An illiterate shepherd, Simon climbed atop a sixty-foot stone pillar that was reputed to have been no more than four feet in diameter. Each day his spiritual exercises consisted of throwing himself on his knees and forehead repeatedly. Curious crowds came to watch, marvel at, and count his prostrations—several reported that he usually did 1,244 "falls" each day before stopping to preach to the crowd from his high perch. According to a writer of the time, Simon

> Retired to a neighboring height, and there marked out for himself a circular enclosure; to prevent himself from passing beyond this enclosure he attached himself to a large stone by a chain, and for four years he stood within the enclosure without lying or sitting down, 'snowed upon, rained upon, and scorched'. His fame spread far and wide; pilgrims came in large numbers; the sick sought healing; all wished to touch him or to carry off some relic from the Saint. The night and the greater part of the day he spent in prayer, but twice a day he addressed the folk who thronged about the column, giving them moral counsel, settling their disputes, healing their diseases.[53]

That the Dendrites and Stylites were very strange is undeniable, yet their lives were effective sermons. Through their prayer, severe form of asceticism, and teaching by example, their suffering became a positive force in a medieval world marked by wars, natural disasters, disease, and murderous crime. High above the ground, alone with God and separated from the world, they paradoxically were able to minister effectively to the world that they had rejected.

SELF-FLAGELLATION

Suffering while at work took a distinct turn in severity during the thirteenth century. Hermits seeking new ways to suffer while at prayer took note of Christ's suffering as he was lead to the cross. Biblical descriptions noted bleeding from his crown of thorns and from the whips of Roman soldiers. Wishing to emulate Christ's suffering, some hermit monks began the practice of self-flagellation as part of their prayer routine.

When the terrible bubonic plague of 1259 began to sweep across Europe and hundreds of thousands of people began dying from the disease, many hermit monks viewed the scourge as evidence for the long-awaited end of the world. There appeared a famous Italian hermit from Umbria, Raniero Fasani, who emerged from his cave to organize a brotherhood of other hermit monks called *Disciplinati di Gesú Cristo,* "Followers of Jesus Christ." This band of hermit monks gained a following as they walked throughout central and northern Italy. The thirteenth-century writer, Jean de Venette, witnessed and recorded one such spectacle:

Two medieval monks perform self-flagellation, a form of penitence designed to emulate the suffering of Christ as he was lead to the cross.

Stripped to the waist, they gathered in large groups and bands and marched in procession through the crossroads and squares of cities and good towns. They formed circles and beat upon their backs with weighted scourges [whips], rejoicing as they did so in loud voices and singing hymns suitable to their rite and newly composed for it. They flogged their shoulders and arms, studded with iron points so zealously as to draw blood. [54]

Flagellants were viewed by some during the Middle Ages as practitioners of excessive zeal in their efforts to suffer while communicating with God. Others, however, accorded them high esteem. In some towns, the clergy and townspeople and even children followed their example in preparation for the end of the world. Great processions, amounting sometimes to ten thousand people, followed the hermit monks as they passed through the cities beating themselves and urging the faithful to pray.

THE CENOBITES

The occasional bizarre behavior of some hermit monks caught the attention of more moderate ones. Concerned that monks living isolated lives might not produce the best thinkers and role models for the secular community, a group of monks believed that more needed to be asked of hermit monks. Independent groups scattered across Europe introduced the idea of gathering hermit monks together into small, loosely constituted communities. Hermits choosing to join were called Cenobites from the Greek *koinos-bios,* meaning those living "collective lives." The One Cenobitic Charter, which was typical of many agreements between monasteries and monks in medieval Europe, demanded a strict adherence to the Rule of Saint Benedict. In particular, the charter emphasized the importance of poverty, admonishing,

Take care that the brethren have everything in common. No one must own as much as a needle. Your body and soul shall be your own, and nothing else. Everything must be shared equally with love between all your spiritual children, brethren and fathers. [55]

Leaders of the Cenobites were in agreement that the work of prayer, asceticism, and teaching by example were qualities worth continuing, along with the additional task of communal work. One of the Cenobite leaders, St. Pachomius, introduced the need for manual labor that would be applied to the feeding of all monks and to the construction of common areas for such activities as eating and sleeping. Noticing that many were illiterate, Pachomius also urged education to be added to the daily work of the monks. Father

❧ COMPETITIVE SUFFERING ☙

Extreme hermits were occasionally known to compete with one another to determine who could endure the greatest amount of suffering. Although the object of suffering was not to make it into a competition, some monks became carried away with it.

One such competitive hermit named Alexander Macarius visited a group of hermits with the intention of outdoing them with his suffering. Without disclosing his true identity, he was admitted into their group. As the celebration of Lent arrived, a time when everyone was to give up some form of comfort, each of the hermits chose to give up food and began to fast.

Some were able to fast for two days, and one even lasted an entire week. Other hermits suffered by standing an entire night in prayer or by burial in a dirt pit for twenty-four hours. After observing these demonstrations of suffering, Macarius decided on his strategy. He went to a corner of a room and remained there praying without food, drink, and sleep.

After two days the other monks began to complain that this stranger was making fools of them. After five days they became enraged demanding that he stop. Finally after one week, he stopped. The embarrassed and angry hermits interrogated him, demanding to know who he was and how he was able to undergo such extreme suffering. When he finally revealed that he was an experienced and well-known ascetic, the other hermits thanked him for teaching them a lesson about humility and then asked him to kindly depart, adding as he left, that he was never to return.

Matthias Farid Wahba, theology instructor at the University of California, Los Angeles, has this to say about Pachomius's contribution:

> He perceived that the life of solitude is not possible for everyone; so he thought to inaugurate a combination of asceticism and cenobitic, or communal life. Perhaps the most revolutionary features in the system were the introduction of manual labor and a considerable measure of education.[56]

In keeping with the tradition of hermit monks, however, each one was still allowed to retreat to a private cave or room for prayer. Unlike monks living in monasteries, Cenobites were free to depart from the community several times during the day, and they were not constricted by the complex system of rules introduced by monks such as St. Benedict and St. Hildemar. As the historian C.K. Lawrence paints the picture,

> These colonies contained several hundred solitaries [monks] living in caves or huts out of sight, and generally out of earshot, of one another. A group of this kind was called a *laura,* a Greek word meaning a pathway or a passage, and apparently derived from the common pathway that connected the caves. [57]

The excessive austerity and single-minded focus on prayer, which had been the cardinal maxim for hermit monks, gradually gave way to a broader set of responsibilities for those willing to pursue the profession of monks. Monks, especially in Western Europe, moved away from living as hermits in favor of the Cenobitic life of a more diverse set of responsibilities.

Such was the evolution and breadth of differences found within the monks' profession. Over a one-thousand-year period, monks experienced a variety of lifestyles, jobs, monastic rules, and commitments to Christianity. Although all monks expressed their devotion in a variety of ways, the one common denominator shared by all was their commitment to prayer and *opus Dei.*

INTRODUCTION: MEN WHO PRAYED

1. Matthew 19:21 RSV.
2. Quoted in C.H. Lawrence, *Medieval Monasticism.* London: Longman, 2001, p. 1.

CHAPTER 1: TRAINING YOUNG MEN TO BECOME MONKS

3. Quoted in Mayke de Jong, "Growing Up in a Carolingian Monastery: Hildemar and His Oblates," *Journal of Medieval History 9,* 1983, p. 115.
4. Mayke de Jong, "Growing Up in a Carolingian Monastery," p. 115.
5. Benedictine College, "The Holy Rule of St. Benedict—Rule XXXV," 2003. www.benedictine.edu.
6. "The Holy Rule of St. Benedict—Rule XXXV."
7. Mayke de Jong, "Growing Up in a Carolingian Monastery," p. 113.
8. "The Holy Rule of St. Benedict—Rule XIX."
9. Quoted in Peter Speed, *Those Who Prayed: An Anthology of Medieval Sources.* New York: Ithaca Press, 1997, p. 157.
10. Mayke de Jong, "Growing Up in a Carolingian Monastery," p. 111.
11. "The Holy Rule of St. Benedict—Rule LXIII."

12. Quoted in Peter Speed, *Those Who Prayed,* p. 157.
13. Quoted in Peter Speed, *Those Who Prayed,* p. 157.
14. "The Holy Rule of St. Benedict—Rule XLV."

CHAPTER 2: SPIRITUAL LABOR

15. Quoted in Steve Peterson, "Suffering in the Service of Christ," *Whosoever,* June 2000. www.whosoever.org.
16. "The Holy Rule of St. Benedict—Rule XX."
17. "The Holy Rule of St. Benedict—Rule LIII."
18. "The Holy Rule of St. Benedict—Rule XXXI."
19. Quoted in Ludo J.R. Milis, *Angelic Monks and Earthly Men: Monasticism and Its Meaning to Medieval Society.* Woodridge, England: Boydell Press, 1992, p. 58.
20. Quoted in C.H. Lawrence, *Medieval Monasticism,* p. 118.
21. Quoted in Paul Halsall, "Medieval Source Book: Anna Comnena: The Alexiad," *Internet Medieval Source Book,* June 1997, www.fordham.edu.
22. Quoted in Peter Speed, *Those Who Prayed,* p. 92.
23. Peter Speed, *Those Who Prayed,* p. 78.
24. Quoted in Peter Speed, *Those Who Prayed,* p. 80.

25. Quoted in C.H. Lawrence, *Medieval Monasticism,* p. 115.
26. Quoted in C.H. Lawrence, *Medieval Monasticism,* p. 115.
27. "The Holy Rule of St. Benedict—Rule XXII."

CHAPTER 3: RUNNING A MONASTERY
28. Translated by the author.
29. "The Holy Rule of St. Benedict—Rule LXVI."
30. C.H. Lawrence, *Medieval Monasticism,* p. 57.
31. Quoted in Geoffrey Baskerville, *English Monks and the Suppression of the Monasteries.* London: Jonathan Cape, 1937, p. 28.
32. "The Holy Rule of St. Benedict—Rule XXXVI."
33. C.H. Lawrence, *Medieval Monasticism,* p. 117.

CHAPTER 4: SCHOLARS
34. Jean Décarreaux, *Monks and Civilization.* Trans. Charlotte Haldane. Garden City, NY: Doubleday, 1964, p. 336.
35. Andrew Dickson White, "A History of the Warfare of Science with Theology in Christendom: New Beginnings of Medical Science," University of Georgia. http://abob.libs.uga.edu/bobk/whitem06.html.

CHAPTER 5: ARTISTS AND MUSICIANS
36. Quoted in Frances and Joseph Gies, *Cathedral, Forge, and Waterwheel.* New York: HarperCollins, 1994, p. 130.
37. Beyond Books, "Painting Before 1300," 2002. www.beyondbooks.com.
38. Caryl Coleman, "Stained Glass," *New Advent,* 2003. www.newadvent.org.
39. Quoted in Erwin Panofsky, "Abbot Suger of Saint-Denis," Columbia University, 1999. www.columbia.edu.

CHAPTER 6: TRAVELING MONKS
40. Quoted in C.H. Lawrence, *Medieval Monasticism,* p. 242.
41. Quoted in "Mendicant Monks," *New Advent,* December 2, 2002. www.newadvent.org.
42. Quoted in Paul Halsall, "Medieval Source Book: Richer of Rheims: Journey to Chartres, Tenth Century," *Internet Medieval Source Book,* June 1997. www.fordham.edu.
43. Quoted in Peter Speed, *Those Who Prayed,* pp. 164–65.
44. Catholic Church in England & Wales, "Pope John Paul II's Letter to Cardinal Hume," May 1997. http://217.19.224.165/frameset.htm.
45. David Ross, "Early Christianity in Britain," *Britain Express,* 2000. www.britainexpress.com.
46. Jean Décarreaux, *Monks and Civilization,* p. 273.
47. Robert Beecham, "The Knights Templar," *History of the Knights Templar,* 2001. www.templarhistory.com.

48. Quoted in Peter Speed, *Those Who Prayed,* p. 195.

CHAPTER 7: HERMIT MONKS

49. Quoted in Philip Schaff and Henry Wace, eds., *Select Works and Letters, Volume IV of Nicene and Post-Nicene Fathers, Series II.* Grand Rapids, MI: William B. Eerdmans, 1984, p. 198.
50. Quoted in Peter Speed, *Those Who Prayed,* p. 23.
51. Quoted in "Crimes of Christianity: Monkery," *Paradise.net* 2002. www. paradise.net.
52. Jacques LaCarrière, *Men Possessed by God: The Story of the Desert Monks of Ancient Christendom.* Trans. Roy Monkcom. Garden City, NY: Doubleday, 1964, p. 153.

53. Quoted in Paul Halsall, "Medieval Source Book: The Life of Daniel the Stylite," *Internet Medieval Source Book,* June 1997, www.fordham.edu.
54. Quoted in Ellis L. Knox, "The Black Death," *ORB: The Online Reference Book for Medieval Studies,* 1991. http://orb.rhodes.edu.
55. Very Reverend Dr. Radomir Popovic, "The One Cenobitic Charter," Serbian Orthodox Church, 2003. www.kosovo.com.
56. Father Matthias Farid Wahba, "The Coptic Orthodox Church of Egypt," UCLA Student Group Web Service, 2001. www.studentgroups.ucla.edu.
57. C.H. Lawrence, *Medieval Monasticism,* p. 5.

FOR FURTHER READING

Robert A. Barakat, *The Cistercian Sign Language: A Study in Non-Verbal Communication.* Kalamazoo, MI: Cistercian Publications, 1975. This book provides a history of sign language used by monks and includes photographs of monks signing hundreds of words and thoughts.

Frances and Joseph Gies, *Cathedral, Forge, and Waterwheel.* New York: HarperCollins. 1994. This book presents a lively discussion about medieval technology that includes information about discoveries made by monks. The authors write of such advances in monasteries as the Gothic flying buttress, primitive water pumps, and the development of stained glass.

Christopher De Hamel, *Medieval Craftsmen: Scribes and Illuminators.* Toronto: University of Toronto Press, 1992. This book provides an excellent history of the copying and illuminating of medieval texts as well as a variety of color photographs of unusual and beautiful manuscripts.

Meredith Lillich, *Studies in Medieval Stained Glass and Monasticism.* London: Pindar Press, 2001. Professor Lillich discusses the development of stained glass in France with a particular focus on monastic crafts-men, characteristics, requirements, and achievements. He discusses the many artisans and techniques necessary to produce stained glass. Beautiful photographs accompany the text.

Marilyn Oliva, *The Convent and the Community in Late Medieval England: Female Monasteries in the Diocese of Norwich, 1350–1540.* Woodbridge, Suffolk, UK: Boydell Press, 1998. In her study of the eleven female monasteries in the diocese of Norwich between 1350–1540, the author describes the convents as integral parts of the local social and spiritual landscape. She also found the nuns to be more active in the local community than their male counterparts and markedly more popular with the local populations.

Conrad Rudolph, *Violence & Daily Life: Reading, Art, and Polemics in the Citeaux "Moralia in Job."* Princeton, NJ: Princeton University Press, 1997. This book discusses a twelfth-century manuscript called *Moralia in Job,* which is a lavishly written and illuminated book depicting life at the Cistercian monastery of Citeaux in the year 1111. It contains many images of violence along with images of normal daily life at the monastery.

WORKS CONSULTED

BOOKS

Geoffrey Baskerville, *English Monks and the Suppression of the Monasteries.* London: Jonathan Cape, 1937. This book focuses on English monasteries by describing the lives of the monks, their duties, and eventual conflict with the secular authority of the kings of England.

Daniel Caner, *Wandering, Begging Monks.* Berkeley, CA: University of California Press, 2002. The author presents a detailed discussion about the variety of monks who wandered throughout medieval Europe while begging for food and praying for their sins. Caner also provides detailed explanations for the origins of this movement.

G.G. Coulton, *Life in the Middle Ages.* Cambridge, England: Cambridge University Press, 1957. This book gives a view of the day-to-day life of people in the Middle Ages with a specific focus on what it was like to live in a medieval village. Much of the evidence for this book comes from archaeological work and from a thorough reading of hundreds of historical texts.

Fred H. Crossley, *The English Abbey.* London: B.T. Batsford Ltd., 1942. This book focuses on the medieval abbeys, monasteries, and convents in England. Primary topics for discussion are the architecture, construction materials and techniques, and the daily lives within each of the three religious structures.

Jean Décarreaux, *Monks and Civilization.* Translated by Charlotte Haldane. Garden City, NY: Doubleday, 1964. This work focuses on the role that monks played in saving and preserving the culture and civilization handed down from the Greeks and Romans that might otherwise have been lost during the Middle Ages.

Geneviéve D'Haucourt, *Life in the Middle Ages.* Translated by Veronica Hull. New York: Sun Books, 1963. This work is intended to illuminate the day-to-day activities in the lives of the people who lived during the Middle Ages. The author draws from primary sources to describe many of the mundane yet fascinating details and experiences about the lives of the nobility, the monks, and the common peasant.

Jacques LaCarrière, *Men Possessed by God: The Story of the Desert Monks of Ancient Christendom.* Translated by Roy Monkcom. Garden City, NY: Doubleday, 1964. The author presents an excellent history of hermit monks, how they came into being, and the various cults that formed around their bizarre lifestyles.

C.H. Lawrence, *Medieval Monasticism.* London: Longman, 2001. This book is a superb scholarly endeavor that is considered one of the best overviews of medieval monasticism. Lawrence is a senior scholar who presents a variety of descriptions and discussions of monks, their place in European history, and their intellectual environments.

Ludo J.R. Milis, *Angelic Monks and Earthly Men: Monasticism and Its Meaning to Medieval Society.* Woodbridge, Suffolk, UK: Boydell Press, 1992. Milis focuses on the value that medieval monks contributed to European culture as scholars, artists, farmers, and doctors.

Philip Schaff and Henry Wace, editors, *Select Works and Letters, Volume IV of Nicene and Post-Nicene Fathers, Series II.* Grand Rapids, MI: William B. Eerdmans, 1984. This book is a compilation of primary sources addressing many aspects of monasticism in Medieval Europe.

Peter Speed, *Those Who Prayed: An Anthology of Medieval Sources.* New York: Ithaca Press, 1997. A source book of carefully selected quotations from medieval source documents highlighting the lives and work of monks.

PERIODICALS

Mayke de Jong, "Growing Up in a Carolingian Monastery: Hildemar and His Oblates," *Journal of Medieval History 9,* 1983.

INTERNET SOURCES

Robert Beecham, "The Knights Templar," *History of the Knights Templar,* 2001. www.templarhistory.com.

Benedictine College, "The Holy Rule of St. Benedict," 2003. www.benedictine.edu.

"Buckfast Monastery," *Information Devon,* 2001. www.devon.gov.uk

Caryl Coleman, "Stained Glass," *New Advent,* 2003, www.newadvent.org.

"Crimes of Christianity: Monkery," *Paradise.net,* 2002. www.paradise.net.

Paul Halsall, "Medieval Source Book: Anna Comnena: The Alexiad," *Internet Medieval Source Book,* June 1997. www.fordham.edu.

Paul Halsall, "Medieval Source Book: The Life of Daniel the Stylite," *Internet Medieval Source Book,* June 1997. www.fordham.edu.

Paul Halsall, "Medieval Source Book: Richer of Rheims: Journey to Chartres, Tenth Century," *Internet Medieval Source Book,* June 1997. www.fordham.edu.

Ellis L. Knox, "The Black Death," *ORB: The Online Reference Book for Medieval Studies,* 1999. http://orb.rhodes.edu.

"Mendicant Monks," *New Advent,* December 2, 2002. www.newadvent. org.

"Painting Before 1300," *Beyond Books,* 2002. www.beyondbooks.com.

Erwin Panofsky, "Abbot Suger of Saint-Denis," Columbia University, 1999. www.columbia.edu.

Steve Peterson, "Suffering in the Service of Christ," *Whosoever,* June 2000. www.whosoever.org.

"Pope John Paul II's Letter to Cardinal Hume," *Catholic Church in England & Wales,* May 1997. http://217.19.224.165/frameset.htm.

Very Reverend Dr. Radomir Popovic, "The One Cenobitic Charter," Serbian Orthodox Church, 2003. www.kosovo.com.

David Ross, "Early Christianity in Britain," *Britain Express,* 2000. www.britainexpress.com.

Father Matthias Farid Wahba, "The Coptic Orthodox Church of Egypt," UCLA Student Group Web Service, 2001. www.studentgroups.ucla.edu.

Andrew Dickson White, "A History of the Warfare of Science with Theology in Christendom: New Beginnings of Medical Science," The University of Georgia. http://abob.libs.uga.edu/bobk/whitem06.html.

Susan Wallace, "Commonly Used Medical Plants," *Exploring the Middle Ages,* 2002. www.skell.org.

WEBSITES

Medieval Source Book (www.fordham.edu). Fordham University Center for Medieval Studies provides this website containing hundreds of documents translated into English. Each document is referenced in one of several dozen topics and contains a brief introduction explaining its importance to medieval history.

New Advent (www.newadvent.org). This website contains an enormous amount of information on the history of the Catholic Church, including encyclopedia entries, definitions of technical works, as well as hundreds of internet links to other electronic sources of information about the Catholic Church.

ORB: The Online Reference Book for Medieval Studies (http://orb.rhodes.edu). ORB is an academic site written and maintained by university medieval scholars to provide primary and secondary source material.

St. Pachomius Library (www.ocf.org). This website provides an extensive collection of documents and links focused on the medieval church.

INDEX

PICTURE CREDITS

ABOUT THE AUTHOR

James Barter received his undergraduate degree in history and classics at the University of California (Berkeley) followed by graduate studies in ancient history and archaeology at the University of Pennsylvania. Mr. Barter has taught history as well as Latin and Greek.

A Fulbright scholar at the American Academy in Rome, Mr. Barter worked on archaeological sites in and around the city as well as on sites in the Naples area. Mr. Barter also has worked and traveled extensively in Greece.

Mr. Barter currently lives in Rancho Santa Fe, California, with his seventeen-year-old daughter, Kalista, who is a senior at Torrey Pines High School, works as a soccer referee, excels at math, physics, and English, and is planning for a career in communications as a freshman at the Annenberg School of Communications at the University of Southern California. Mr. Barter's older daughter, Tiffany, and her husband, Mike, live where she teaches violin and performs in classical music recitals.